SEEING
IN THE SPIRIT
MADE SIMPLE

SEEING
IN THE SPIRIT
MADE SIMPLE

Praying Medic

**INKITY
PRESS**™

Inkity Press™
137 East Elliot Road, #2292, Gilbert, AZ 85234

This book and other Inkity Press titles can be found at:
InkityPress.com and PrayingMedic.com

Available from Amazon.com, CreateSpace.com, and other retail outlets.

For more information visit our website at **www.inkitypress.com**
or email us at **admin@inkitypress.com** or **admin@prayingmedic.com**

ISBN-13: 978-0692427927 (Inkity Press)
ISBN-10: 0692427929

Printed in the U.S.A.

I'D LIKE TO DEDICATE THIS book to my wife, who has been my best friend and closest companion on my journey into the Kingdom of God. It was her desire to learn to see in the spirit that caused me to seek the Lord's counsel about the process, and which gave us the revelation we're now able to share with you.

························
ACKNOWLEDGMENTS

I WOULD LIKE TO THANK the many people who helped in the development of this book by providing feedback during my public discussions and by leaving comments on the articles I've posted. You know who you are. I greatly value your experiences, your insights and your encouragement.

I'd like to thank Jeremy Mangerchine, Jesse Birkey and Michael VanVlymen for their support of the concept of this book and their feedback on first drafts of the manuscript. I'd like to thank Matt Evans, Steve Harmon and Michael King for their insights and testimonies. I'd also like to thank David McLain and Todd Adams for their daily love and encouragement toward me.

I'd like to thank my talented wife for her editorial help with the manuscript and for her design of the book interior and cover.

There is some difficulty involved in making the abstract ideas of the spiritual world more real and concrete. I'm grateful to my editor and friend Lydia Blain for asking all the right questions and insisting that

I clarify points that seemed unclear. If this book helps you to better understand the spiritual world, it is largely due to her skill as a writing coach. If you need help editing your project (regardless of how big or small the project is) you're welcome to contact her through her website: www.lydiaedits.com

~ Praying Medic

TABLE OF CONTENTS

NOTE

Although I work as a trained paramedic, I am not a physician. I cannot diagnose diseases or recommend the best course of medical treatment for them. The advice given in this book is not intended to replace the advice of a medical doctor or other licensed health care professional. I do not assume liability for any harm that results from a decision to forego medical treatment. I cannot guarantee that the suggestions given in this book will result in the same outcomes I, or others, have experienced. I am not responsible for the outcomes that result from following the advice given in this book. There is no guarantee that the teaching in this book will lead to healing. While I believe wholeheartedly in divine healing, I also believe in and encourage you to seek standard diagnostic testing and medical treatment if it is indicated.

CHAPTER ONE

Drawing Near to God

DURING THE COURSE OF WRITING this book, I had a conversation with a man who has walked with the Lord much longer than I have. In spite of this, he doesn't have the type of experiences with God that I do. He asked for my thoughts on why he wasn't seeing people miraculously healed or why he wasn't able to see visions. He attended Bible school and has held different positions in church leadership over the years. He has a thorough knowledge of the scriptures and provided sound theological answers to the questions I asked him. His answers were the kind you would expect to hear if you were taking a test on theology. They were the right answers doctrinally, though few seemed to have any experiential knowledge behind them. His trouble (or so he thought) was that God had excluded him from the inner circle of people who are allowed to have supernatural experiences and he wanted to know what reason God might have for keeping him from having them.

I thought that perhaps he was looking at the problem from the wrong perspective, and I suggested that it was actually him and not God who was limiting his experiences. He replied with another theological truth he had picked up somewhere along the way. As with many of his replies, it deflected my question and we never got to the bottom of the issue. I think the problem is that my friend is afraid to take an honest look at his own responsibilities in his relationship with God.

Our view of God has a tremendous influence on the kind of experiences we have with Him. Some people see God as an austere deity who is too busy to be troubled with their personal problems. For them, God is very distant, relationally. They don't allow themselves the privilege of experiencing the intimacy and love of the Father. Others see God as their best friend, closest confidant, and spiritual lover. Their days are filled with intimate experiences with the Creator God. It's tempting to think that God is the one who sets the stage for our relationship, but it is actually our personal view of Him that dictates the experiences we have. If we permit ourselves the liberty of seeing Him as a friend, we'll have the kind of experiences that friends have. If we see Him as too busy to be bothered, we'll never feel worthy of being in His presence.

The relationships that are the most meaningful are the ones where we're free to be ourselves with the other party. This means we must take the risk of being transparent, and trust that they will not reject us when they learn about the things we're not proud of. If we refuse to let them see our deepest secrets, we prevent the relationship from growing.

There is a tendency in the church to view God somewhat like Isaiah did when he encountered the glory of the Lord in the temple. Many of us envision Him as being so holy and unapproachable, and ourselves so depraved and unclean that we fear drawing near to Him. At least that's how our theology might tell us to see God. What we often fail to realize is that at the cross, our depravity and uncleanness was removed from us forever and we were given a new nature and new clothing that allows us to draw near to Him in the same way a child would sit in the lap of the most adoring father. All that ever separated us from enjoying His company has been removed, and if we fail to enter into an intimate relationship with Him, it is not because we are unworthy of His companionship. It is because we see ourselves as being unworthy and out of fear, refuse to draw near to Him, preferring to cling to views of ourselves and Him that are misguided theological constructs that bear no resemblance to how things actually are. Like anyone else having a relationship problem, it's easier for us to think it is the other party who is holding things back instead of admitting that we are the one who refuses to move the relationship forward.

My wife had been struggling with the burden of deciding what steps to take next in her career. She is trained as a painter and her heart's desire is to paint the pictures that flow from her imagination, but the stereotype she learned in art school about starving artists always prevented her from believing she could make a living as a painter. So for the last 15 years she's worked as a graphic designer because it pays the bills. The work doesn't inspire her and it often leaves her with neck pain and a headache at the end of the day, but she's been afraid of making the changes that would allow her to become a full-time painter. The real struggle is that she wasn't certain what God wanted her to do. She felt if she made the wrong choice, she might disappoint God, never sell any paintings, and leave us in a difficult place, financially.

One night she had a dream where Jesus paid her a visit. In the dream, He came to her rather excitedly and handed her a piece of paper. The paper was blank except for the letterhead at the top that appeared in a beautiful pink font which read: "Super Praying Medic's Wife." After handing her the blank piece of paper, He looked excitedly into her eyes and asked, "What are you going to be?"

This dream profoundly changed the way in which my wife saw her relationship with Jesus. Rather than thinking she had to somehow know what He wanted her to do (and suffer the consequences if she was wrong) she realized that He was actually her biggest fan, and that regardless of which choice she made, He supported her decision and was excited to see how it would turn out. The dream destroyed a lot of bad theology she had picked up on her journey through life and replaced it with a more accurate portrait of God—one based on a personal encounter she had with Him.

As you read about the personal encounters my wife and I have had, consider the fact that God wants to have the same type of encounters with all of us, even you. If you're afraid to approach God because you feel unworthy to be in His presence, try seeing yourself the way He sees you, and not how others have seen you. If you have discomfort at the thought of drawing near to your heavenly Father because your earthly father made you feel uncomfortable, please understand that God the Father is nothing like any earthly father you've ever met. You are the apple of His eye and like the prodigal's father, He is waiting to lavish you with His love and affection, but you must make the first move. It is we who place most of the limits on our experiences with God. As you draw near to Him, you will find that He really will draw near to you.

CHAPTER TWO

Why Do We Need Another Book on Seeing in the Spirit?

SEEING IN THE SPIRIT IS an enigma to most people. For those who regularly see angels, demons, and other spirit beings, it's as natural as breathing. But for most people, just trying to define what we mean by the phrase "seeing in the spirit" is problematic. For the sake of clarity, in this book, I'll be referring to a set of experiences collectively as "seeing in the spirit." Those experiences include things like dreams and the appearance of angels, demons, and other spirit beings. I would also include in the definition such things as trances and visions. Anything that we see—with our natural eyes or our spiritual ones—that does not have its reality based in the physical world would be considered seeing in the spirit. We may also be shown things that exist in the physical world (such as distant planets) that are impossible to see with the naked eye. When something is made plainly visible to us that would otherwise be impossible to see, it would be considered seeing in the spirit, since our ability to perceive it requires supernatural vision.

Although several decent books have been written on the subject of seeing in the spirit in recent years—and I consider a few of the authors to be friends of mine—I disagree with some of the main points that are being taught on this subject. I do not believe that seeing in the spirit is a gift which is only given to a few people, a special anointing you must seek, or something you must receive by impartation from a well-known teacher. I believe that seeing in the spirit is an innate ability we all have, which simply needs to be developed through exercise.

In my book *Divine Healing Made Simple* I wrote about the fact that in recent days, God had raised up an army of average people who were operating in supernatural healing in everyday settings. For years, the realm of healing had mostly been confined to a handful of professional ministers. The long-held belief that healing is a gift reserved only for a few special individuals prevented people from operating in divine healing. In my book, I put forward the argument that with a little knowledge and practice, divine healing can be done by any Christian. Today God is working miracles through truck drivers, accountants, plumbers, baristas, mechanics, stay-at-home moms, and paramedics—people with no formal religious training or education. This recent move of God has given back spiritual significance to the type of people Jesus chose as His first disciples. All the books that I write are intended to demonstrate the fact that God can do extraordinary things through ordinary people. This book will demonstrate the fact that virtually anyone can see in the spirit, regardless of their background, education, or spiritual qualifications.

It is my belief that you don't need to be a spiritual super-star to see visions and have dreams. The average person who works a regular job and doesn't have a lot of free time on their hands can see in the spirit as accurately as anyone else. If you were to have lunch with me, chances are you'd find me to be a very ordinary person. I had a pretty normal childhood. I don't attend a lot of spiritual conferences or prayer meetings. I don't spend much time soaking in God's presence. For the last fifteen years I've averaged 50 to 60 hours a week at a full-time job. Most days I come home too tired to do anything except grab a bite to eat with my wife before going to bed. To be perfectly honest, I'm just too busy to set aside several hours a day to pray. I'm not what you would call a spiritual giant.

In spite of all this, I've been seeing in the spirit for several years, though it wasn't always this way. I wasn't born with a fully-developed ability to do this. Until just a few years ago, I had never seen a vision from God. My ability to see in the spirit had to be developed over time, and if someone like me can learn to do it, so can you. Other books on seeing in the spirit may leave you feeling like God hasn't chosen you to be a "seer" or hasn't given you this "gift." It's my belief that virtually anyone can learn this ability. The goal of this book is to provide a path anyone can follow to develop this ability.

CHAPTER THREE

Objections to Seeing in the Spirit

THE PROPHETS AND APOSTLES RECEIVED much of their revelation from God in the form of dreams, visions, trances, and angelic messages. This revelation has been preserved for us in the pages of scripture. I'll provide examples and illustrations from the lives of Old and New Testament authors describing how they received their revelation. As we examine their lives, it is my hope that the biblical basis for seeing in the spirit will become abundantly clear. In this chapter, I'll deal primarily with the objections people have raised about seeing in the spirit.

For the sake of simplicity, in this chapter, I'll refer to the various forms of visionary experiences— visions, dreams, trances, and angelic messages—collectively as "special revelation." I can't address all of the objections that have been raised against people receiving special revelation; however, I would like to address the ones that you are most likely to encounter.

Special Revelation Leads to Deception

One objection comes from the observation that some people have been greatly deceived by what they've learned through special revelation. A classic example is Joseph Smith, the prophet of Mormonism, who was given special revelation from the angel Moroni that became the basis for his teachings, which are viewed by most Christians as being dangerously heretical. Pointing to examples such as this, many church leaders sternly warn their congregations that only deception and heresy can come from seeking special revelation.

While it is true that some people have been deceived through special revelation, others received revelation containing important keys to God's plan. The apostle Peter would never have brought the gospel to the Gentiles were it not for the revelation he received while in a trance, and the apostle Paul would not have visited Macedonia, except for the revelation he received in a night vision (see Acts chapter 10 and Acts 16:9-10).

The fact that some have been deceived through special revelation does not mean that all people will be deceived by it. The logic being used here is the belief that if it happens to one person, it will happen to all. If this were true, it would logically follow that no one should ever drive a car again because thousands of people a year are killed in car accidents. We don't prohibit driving simply because it poses a few risks to drivers and passengers. The responsible thing to do is to make driving as safe as possible by taking a few precautions: Wear a seat belt. Drive the speed limit. Don't pass another car when it's not safe. Don't drive drunk.

Are there dangers involved in seeking special revelation?

Of course there are dangers. There are many deceiving spirits at work today that are more than willing to provide false information to unsuspecting seekers. But there are also legitimate messages being sent by God that contain true revelation. Some people are afraid to assume any type of risk in their spiritual life, while others know that in order to advance the kingdom of God we must be willing to take certain risks. Wise believers know that there are ways to minimize or eliminate exposure to risk. Instead of prohibiting special revelation, we must learn how to discern the true from the false. When we receive revelation through visions, trances and angelic encounters, before we accept it, we must run it through various filters: Test the spirits, compare the revelation we receive with the scriptures, compare it with what we know about God, consult with trusted leaders, and learn how to evaluate the fruit that comes from it. If we do these things there is no reason to fear that we will be deceived.

Usurping the Authority of Scripture

Another common objection is the fear that if special revelation were to be received, people may attempt to add it to the canon of scripture or use it to replace the teachings of the Bible.

This fear may in fact be valid, and there are undoubtedly those who are foolish enough to use special revelation to replace the teachings of scripture. But we must ask if it is wise and prudent to negate the validity of all special revelation simply because a few people would place more emphasis on it than they should.

It is neither wise nor prudent to prohibit all special revelation simply because some choose to over-emphasize its importance. The solution is to learn how to discern the true from the false, and to rightly prioritize it. We should not think that we don't need the Bible, just because we can receive revelation directly from God. I rely heavily upon my own dreams for personal direction, but the scriptures are indispensable as a tool to help me interpret and apply the revelation I receive directly from God. We need both if we want to live in the fullness of what He has planned for us.

No Further Revelation

Another objection is the belief that once the canon of scripture was completed that God had no intention of revealing anything further about His plans or His nature directly to man. This view teaches that everything God had to say to us can be found in the Bible, that we need no further revelation, and that God is no longer speaking to man. Adherents to this view believe that if we were to receive any special revelation, it could only come from the kingdom of darkness. This commonly-held belief is contradicted by the words of Jesus in John chapter 16:

> *I still have many things to say to you, but you cannot bear them now. However, when He, the Spirit of truth, has come, He will guide you into all truth; for He will not speak on His own authority, but whatever He hears He will speak; and He will tell you things to come. He will glorify Me, for He will take of what is Mine and declare it to you. All things that the Father has are Mine. Therefore I said that He will take of Mine and declare it to you.*
> JN 16:12-14

It's evident from this passage that Jesus intended to give His disciples further revelation through the Holy Spirit. This book is my attempt to teach believers how to receive the revelation that Jesus said He would give them.

Biblical Examples

Some teach that the supernatural events found in the Bible are not examples for us to follow, but special events that God did not intend to repeat. This view teaches that Jesus only healed and raised the dead because He was God and that we cannot do the same things, because we are not God. This view is hard to accept when we consider the fact that Jesus said His disciples would do the works that He did and even greater works (see Jn 14:12). The Bible itself says that the things we read about in the scriptures were intended to be examples for us. Some examples are ones that we should follow, while others are examples we should not follow (see 1 Cor 10:1-11).

Adherents to this view believe that the events that happened on the day of Pentecost were a one-time occurrence, and not an experience that Christians can have today. Before He ascended into heaven, Jesus told His disciples to wait in Jerusalem for the promise of the Father telling them, *"But you shall receive power when the Holy Spirit has come upon you; and you shall be witnesses to Me..."* (see Acts 1:4, 8). On the day of

Pentecost, when the Holy Spirit fell upon believers and they began to speak in tongues and prophesy, the apostle Peter said:

> *But this is what was spoken by the prophet Joel:*
>
> *And it shall come to pass in the last days, says God,*
> *That I will pour out of My Spirit on all flesh;*
> *Your sons and your daughters shall prophesy,*
> *Your young men shall see visions,*
> *Your old men shall dream dreams.*
> *And on My menservants and on My maidservants*
> *I will pour out My Spirit in those days;*
> *And they shall prophesy.*
> ACTS 2:17-18

According to Peter, we've been living in the fulfillment of this prophecy ever since the day of Pentecost. The fulfillment of this prophecy indicates that when God poured out His Spirit upon His people, all of them (young and old, male and female) would have dreams, see visions, and prophesy. These three things are a few of the ways in which we can receive special revelation from God. These passages indicate that special revelation would not be exclusive to the writers of the scriptures, but that it would be available to all disciples of Jesus throughout the ages. The things that happened on Pentecost not only can, but should be part of the normal experience for every believer. It was normal for the disciples to heal the sick, cast out demons, raise the dead, prophesy, and receive revelation from God through visions, trances, and from angels, and it is no different for us today.

Most of the objections to receiving special revelation are an attempt to put up safeguards and restrictions that are intended to protect people from their own foolishness. While I don't doubt that people who raise these objections have good intentions, I believe there are better solutions than the restrictions they propose. If the main problem we're dealing with is foolishness, the solution to the problem is wisdom. The answer is not to make all special revelation off limits, but to teach believers how to be wise and discerning in spiritual things so that when they're given revelation that is suspicious, they'll be able to rightly discern where it came from, and know what to do with it.

CHAPTER FOUR

Seeing in the Spirit: Gift or Ability?

MOST OF THE BOOKS CURRENTLY available on this subject take the view that seeing in the spirit is either a special anointing from God that we must seek, or a gift from the Holy Spirit that is only given to a few individuals. Some authors refer to seeing in the spirit as the "seer anointing" while others call it a "gift" or an "impartation." While I don't dispute the fact that the Holy Spirit does anoint some people for certain things, and that He gives gifts that are not innate abilities that we possess, I do not believe that seeing in the spirit falls into any of these categories. The idea that seeing in the spirit is a gift from God or a special anointing is not explicitly taught anywhere in the Bible. This belief is mostly based on assumptions drawn from a few obscure passages of scripture that I'll discuss shortly.

A gift speaks of something we cannot do of ourselves. When God specifically grants us the ability to do something, it is considered to be a gift. An example is the gift of tongues. Although you might be able to imitate this gift by speaking in a way that sounds like the gift of tongues, the power that flows through an individual as God enables them to operate in this gift cannot be imitated or conjured up by man. The angels of God may even respond to the legitimate gift of tongues, but they will not respond to the imitation. The gift of tongues is not an innate skill we are born with that can be developed. We refer to it as a "gift" because it cannot be done except by the power of God.

Another example of a gift is the "word of knowledge." A word of knowledge is supernatural revelation given by the Holy Spirit about a situation you would not otherwise know about. You might be able to guess that a person has an injured hip, but the ability to guess correctly carries with it no certainty and no power. If you guess often enough about injuries people have, you'll end up being wrong as often as you're right. When you receive a word of knowledge about a hip injury, you have a degree of certainty that isn't possible with guessing, and you have access to the power of God that will heal the injury. A word of knowledge is called a gift, because it requires the anointing of God in order for it to function.

By contrast, abilities are things we can develop without receiving special empowerment from God before we can do them. We are all born with the innate ability to walk, even though we're not born with the ability fully-developed. We must practice walking before we can do it correctly. You will never hear someone say, "That person has an incredible gift of walking!" Walking does not require a special empowerment from God before we can do it. It requires practice. I'm sure that infants might be tempted to think they will never be able to walk like mom or dad, but once they've practiced enough, they'll be able to walk without falling.

Another example is the ability to play a musical instrument. All humans have the ability to play musical instruments. Like walking, the ability to play an instrument must be developed through practice. We might struggle to believe that we have any musical ability at all when we see someone who has a well-developed ability. While it's true that some people have highly-developed abilities, it's not as if practice will not improve our ability. It's just that some people improve more quickly than others. If we never practice, our ability remains undeveloped, but it is still an ability we possess. Abilities are commonly distributed to all of mankind, even if they are not equally developed.

If seeing in the spirit is a special empowerment from God or a gift that the Holy Spirit only gives to a few people, then we must ask why it is that New Agers and Satanists operate so well in it. Are we to believe that the Holy Spirit distributes these gifts to people who do not know Him? If your answer is that Satan imitates what God does, and that in these cases, they received their gift from him, I might agree with you, but then we must admit that seeing in the spirit is not a gift that only God can give. This line of reasoning compels us to admit that Satan can also give it to whomever he wants. We must also explain why people with absolutely no religious preference at all have the ability to see in the spirit with incredible accuracy. The belief that seeing in the spirit is a special gift or anointing given exclusively by God to certain individuals cannot account for the wide variety of people who operate in it.

The belief that seeing in the spirit is reserved for only a few people has pervaded virtually every part of society. There's a scene in the movie *Thunderheart* that illustrates this fact. In the movie, Val Kilmer's character Ray Levoi is an FBI agent sent to investigate a murder that happened on Sioux tribal land. Ray slowly begins to learn about his identity as a Native American, when he tells the local Indian police officer, Walter Crow Horse, about an experience that he had:

Ray: Just before they caught Jimmy, I had a dream. I was running with other Indians at the Wounded Knee Cemetery. I was shot in the back.

Walter: You were running with the old ones at The Knee?

Ray: It was just a dream.

Walter: Who the hell are you, man?

Ray: What do you mean?

Walter: You had yourself a vision. A man waits a long time to have a vision, and he may go his whole life without having one. Then along comes some instant Indian with a Rolex and a brand new pair of shoes. A damn FBI to top it all off, has himself a vision.

There is certainly a mystique about visions that makes it seem as if only a few people will ever have them. The belief that seeing in the spirit is only for a few people tends to create a two-tiered system, in which a few gifted individuals receive special revelation, which they dispense to those who don't have the gift, in exchange for a fee or recognition. This is how the New Age community operates. Those with the "gift" of seeing dispense supernatural revelation to those without the gift for a fee. Segments of the church have also adopted this model. Prophetically gifted people have taken to dispensing the revelation they receive through visions in exchange for donations and accolades from their supporters. In doing so, we've developed a system that places certain people in places of higher spiritual standing than others.

Under this model, those who have a well-developed ability to see in the spirit seldom consider training those who don't. The ability to see in the spirit is assumed to be a gift and thus, it is also assumed that it cannot be taught to others. The Bible teaches that it's the responsibility of new covenant prophets to train and equip believers for the work of ministry (see Eph. 4:11). Some prophets have tried to teach others about seeing in the spirit, but this generally involves identifying people who already have a well-developed ability and teaching them how to use it properly. Few leaders have tried to help those with a poorly-developed ability to improve their spiritual vision. It's not really the fault of leaders that so little has been done to train and equip believers to see in the spirit. They've been working all this time with a model that gives them no reason to try.

From the beginning of time, when He first spoke into the emptiness and the creation came forth, God has never stopped speaking. Although some people find it hard to recognize His voice, and think He is not speaking to them, the fact is that He is always, eternally speaking to His creation. The problem isn't that God is not speaking. The problem is that He is a Spirit, who speaks in a spiritual language that is received by our spirit, and many of us have not developed our ability to perceive what He is saying. Most of us have had our spiritual senses dulled by sensory input from the physical world, which makes it difficult to recognize input from the spiritual world. The key to perceiving and understanding spiritual communication is to have our spiritual senses trained and refocused. I believe most people receive visions from God on a regular basis, but they're either not aware that what they're seeing is from Him—and they attribute it to their own imagination—or they're not paying attention at all to the visual images He sends them.

The truth is anyone can receive their own revelation directly from God. The benefit is that their relationship with Him would be strengthened. But in our busy culture, it takes time, concentration, and a bit of practice to learn how to receive, interpret, and apply spiritual revelation, and many people find it more convenient to let others do it for them. Part of the problem with a culture that isn't seeing in the spirit or hearing God's voice is spiritual laziness and apathy. The fact that you can receive revelation from God from someone else does not remove your responsibility to learn how to hear Him for yourself. A major part of the process of growing in spiritual maturity is taking responsibility for receiving your own revelation directly from God.

A few people are born with a very sharp ability to see what is going on in the spiritual world. They have the ability to see the realm of demons and angels just as easily as the rest of us see the physical world. The problem for these people is that they must learn to shut out the things they see in the spiritual world, or they'll have difficulty functioning in the physical one. But for most people, the problem is reversed; they're not tuned into the spiritual world, so they must learn how to shut out the physical world in order to focus more on the spiritual one. It's my belief that those who are born with a fully-developed ability to see in the spirit are born that way so that they might help others who need to have their spiritual eyes trained and refocused. For those who are able to see in the spirit, such as prophets, training and equipping the saints involves instruction on how to see in the spirit.

The "Seer"

A common term used today to refer to people who see in the spirit is the word "seer." The use of this term comes from a couple of passages in the Old Testament. The first mention of it is found in 1 Samuel 9:9

which mentions parenthetically, the fact that prophets of the Lord were once called "seers":

(Formerly in Israel, when a man went to inquire of God, he spoke thus: 'Come, let us go to the seer'; for he who is now called a prophet was formerly called a seer).

This passage simply states that the ancient custom was to call a prophet a "seer." If the rule of first mention in scripture is to be taken into account, then the use of the word as an antiquated expression would indicate that "seer" is not a special position or title. It's simply a term that was once used interchangeably for the word "prophet." But the Old Testament does mention both "prophets" and "seers" in the same verse and it seems to make a distinction between them:

Yet the LORD testified against Israel, and against Judah, by all the prophets (nabiy), *and by all the seers* (chozeh).
2 KGS 17:13

From this passage, one could assume that there is a special anointing for the seer that is somehow different from that of the prophet, but this idea is not explicitly taught in the scriptures, so it must be inferred. It's not unusual today to hear people refer to a certain man or woman as a "seer" or as a "seer prophet," which is a special designation for prophets who are believed to have a gift that not all prophets have. The intent of this practice is to create functional descriptions that describe how people operate in ministry. The unintended consequence is that it creates higher and lower levels of spiritual attainment in the church and a kind of caste system that provides privilege and recognition for a few special people. The irony in all of this is that we seem to have lost our understanding of what God originally intended with regard to receiving revelation from Him.

In the beginning, it was God's desire to communicate with all of mankind, personally. It was never His desire to speak to us through someone else. Adam and Even did not have prophets who heard God for them. The use of prophets to speak to man was not God's idea. It was man's idea—and it was a compromise God made because the people of Israel were afraid to commune with Him in person. After they received God's commandments from the mountain, the Israelites told Moses they did not want God to speak to them directly, but only through him:

When the people heard the thunder and the loud blast of the ram's horn, and when they saw the flashes of lightning and the smoke billowing from the mountain, they stood at a distance, trembling with fear.

And they said to Moses, "You speak to us, and we will listen. But don't let God speak directly to us, or we will die!"

"Don't be afraid," Moses answered them, "for God has come in this way to test you, and so that your fear of him will keep you from sinning!"

As the people stood in the distance, Moses approached the dark cloud where God was.
EX 20:18-21 NLT

This encounter set God's people at a distance from Him relationally, and it grew worse as time went on. First they would not hear God directly, but only through a prophet. Later, they would not even heed the voice of the prophets when they spoke. The new covenant, if it is to be better than the old covenant, must abolish the old practices that were never God's desire, and it must replace them with what He originally intended: Face-to-face, spirit-to-spirit communication between two beings that are in love. Our continuation of the practice of relying on certain anointed people to hear God for us must come to an end if we're ever going to grow into mature sons and daughters of God.

Although the Bible refers to many different things as "gifts" there is no mention in scripture of a "gift" of seeing in the spirit. It may actually be considered more of an ability than a gift. Having said that, many of the true spiritual gifts seem to require one or more of our abilities to be developed before they can be used. The gift of discerning of spirits mentioned in 1 Cor. 12:10 is an example.

The discerning of spirits can be done in a number of ways. Some people smell the presence of spirits such as angels or demons, while others can see them. If God intends for you to operate in the gift of discerning spirits by seeing them, you must develop the ability to see in the spirit before you can operate in this gift. The same is true for operating in the gift of the word of knowledge. There are many different ways in which we can receive a word of knowledge. One of them is by seeing something in a vision. If God wants to give you information in the form of a vision, you must first develop your ability to see in the spirit, otherwise it would be impossible for you to receive the information He wants to give you.

While the control of a spiritual gift is subject to the operation of the Holy Spirit, the development of an ability is controlled by the individual. My ability to play guitar is dependent on how much I practice. My ability to see in the spirit is likewise dependent on how much I practice seeing things in the spiritual world. Abilities are honed and perfected through practice and they lie undeveloped when we ignore them. If we never develop our ability to see in the spirit, the operation of the gift of discerning of spirits or the word of knowledge can be hindered.

It is not so much the ability itself that certain people are given, but rather an advanced stage of development of the ability. The fact that someone does not function well in a certain ability doesn't mean the ability isn't there. We all have relatively similar abilities, due to the way in which we are made. But some people receive certain abilities fully-developed, while others receive the same abilities in an undeveloped state. We all have the same potential ability to see in the spirit. Some of us are able to use the ability immediately, while others require some training before they can operate in it.

The writer of the book of Hebrews, speaking about having our spiritual senses trained, said, "But solid food belongs to those who are of full age, that is, those who by **reason of use** have their **senses exercised** to discern both good and evil" (see Heb 5:14—emphasis mine). The author points out that spiritual maturity comes by exercising our senses. Anyone can develop spiritual abilities and gifts through instruction and exercise.

A number of people who have developed their ability to see in the spirit relate stories of having their vision go through sudden, dramatic changes. Some began seeing what appeared to be waves of heat. Some reported seeing objects that appeared to be melting. Others reported seeing objects and beings flickering in and out of existence. While these sudden changes have been attributed to receiving a prophetic impartation, a special anointing from God, or a spiritual gift, the vast majority of people do not have these experiences. For the majority, the changes are not dramatic, but gradual. They simply learn to see in the spirit more accurately by spending time focusing their mind on the unseen world. Seeing in the spirit is not a matter of gifting or anointing, but a matter of focus and practice. That's the way it happened for me and it seems to be the most common path people take.

Developing My Spiritual Vision

In August of 2008, God appeared to me in a dream and said He was going to show me what was wrong with my patients, and that if I prayed with them, He would heal them. Prior to that night, I had never seen a vision and had not had a dream in more than 25 years. (I'll discuss the events of that night in detail in a later chapter.) I wasn't born with a fully-developed ability to see in the spirit, and I didn't know how God was going to show me what was wrong with my patients. But I wanted to see the things He wanted to show me. I needed to take a little initiative and allow my spiritual senses to be trained. Since I didn't have a lot of free time at home, I had to make the best use of my free time at work. Winter is the slow season for EMS where I work. Although we run six or seven calls a day during summer, our call volume drops to one or two calls a day in winter. This provided some time between calls that I could use to have my spiritual vision developed.

God is a relational being and it's impossible to have a meaningful relationship with Him if you won't devote the time needed to develop it. Time is the commodity of relationships, and there really is no way around the issue of spending time with God. I've noticed that when I desire to spend more time with Him, He always finds a way to free up time in my schedule to meet that desire, and that was the case here. God allowed me some free time on duty so that I might use it to get to know Him better, and in the process develop my ability to see in the spirit. If you want to develop this ability and grow closer to God, you'll need to find some time in which to do it. Some people have large blocks of time available every day or several times a week to spend with God, but not everyone does. It isn't necessary to devote an hour or two every day to be alone with God. If you can only spend fifteen minutes a day focusing on Jesus and what He wants to reveal to you—it can make a huge difference.

During that winter, I spent my time between calls sitting alone with my eyes closed on the bench seat in the back of my ambulance. During these times I quieted my soul and did my best to block out distractions from the world around me. I focused my heart on God and gave Him all of my attention. I would often listen to worship music on my iPod as I rested in the back of the ambulance. For the first few days that I did this, I saw very little in the way of visions, but as time went on, I gradually began to see faintly detectable images appear in my mind's eye. There was nothing dramatic about the process. Everything happened very gradually.

At first, the images I saw were blurry and two-dimensional in appearance. They were mostly images of famous people that I recognized. I was finally seeing visions and I was pretty excited, but soon my excitement turned to frustration, because I didn't understand what any of it meant. God doesn't give us visions for our entertainment (although some of the things He'll show you can be pretty amusing). They are usually an invitation to a discussion about something. When you see an image in your mind and you think it might be from Him, it's a good idea to begin a discussion by asking Him what it means. Actually, He already started the discussion by showing you the vision, all you're doing is responding to His invitation to talk.

So I began having a dialogue in my mind with God about the images He showed me. The dialogue consisted of me thinking thoughts in my mind in response to the images I saw. Now this might sound a little crazy if you're not familiar with the process of speaking to God through thoughts, but this is the most common way in which people have conversations with Him. He seldom speaks to people in a loud, booming voice. It's normally done through barely perceptible thought impressions. And since that's how He speaks to us, it's fine for us to speak to Him in the same way.

As I closed my eyes, I would see an image appear. I would silently tell God what I thought it represented. If I guessed correctly, the image would disappear and another image would take its place. If I guessed incorrectly, the image would remain there and I would take another guess at its meaning. Some images required many guesses before I was able to correctly identify what they meant. Some were easy to guess on the first try. Through this process of guessing what each image meant, God was training my spiritual eyes to receive revelation, He was training my mind to display the images accurately, and He was training my heart to understand the visual language He wanted us to use.

As time went on, the images I saw became more sharply focused, and the intensity of the colors was more vivid than what I was able to see even with my physical eyes. The colors of the spiritual realm are nearly infinite. The more you develop your ability to see in the spirit, the more you'll notice increasing intensity and variety of color.

Some of the images I began seeing were translucent in appearance. One feature of the spiritual world is that many things—heavenly ones in particular—radiate a kind of light that is not present in the physical world. (I'll discuss that in more detail in the next chapter.) As I practiced seeing in the spirit, some of the images I saw became three-dimensional and I began seeing multiple scenes that overlapped, and eventually the images began to move. Some of the scenes God showed me were animated cartoons. These visions are something like watching a video in your mind. Moving images and scenes that appear as videos are able to convey a greater depth of meaning than a single image.

Day after day, month after month, I spent most of my spare time at work with my eyes closed, focusing on what God wanted to show me. The more time I spent in training, the better my spiritual vision became and the more I was able to understand the meaning of what I saw. Before long, I was operating with a pretty well-developed ability to see in the spirit—one that I always had, but had never used. It was as if God had planted the seed in me, but I had to water and tend it in order for it to mature and produce fruit. This principle is true of anything you want to develop greater skill at, whether it's playing piano, singing, painting, fishing, healing the sick, or seeing in the spirit. We all have the potential to do these things, but the key to actually doing them is practice.

Warnings

I would be doing readers a disservice if I did not warn them about a few potential problems that come with seeing in the spirit. The first is the fact that not all Christians are going to welcome your discussions about seeing things in the spiritual world. A large part of the body of Christ doesn't believe that God allows us to have these experiences. It's not just that they don't see visions themselves. Many Christians believe that anyone who claims to see things in the spirit is deceived. If you talk about seeing angels and describe heavenly scenes around these people, you can expect to be scolded, rebuked, and excluded from group activities. If the leaders of a church find out about your experiences, you may be asked not to attend their church any longer. If you plan to share what God is showing you, it's imperative to find safe people to discuss your experiences with. Try to find a group of believers who are familiar with these things—mature saints who will listen to your stories without condemnation and who will be able to provide wise counsel and encouragement. It may take a bit of searching, but it will be worth the effort.

It's common to desire these experiences, but it's possible to desire them for the wrong reasons. When you share stories about what you see in the spiritual realm, you can draw a crowd that will hang on your every word. You can go to churches and give prophetic words and receive a lot of money from patrons who will be impressed by your spirituality. People will offer to fly you across the country, at their expense, to have you lay hands on them for healing. Curiosity, popularity, financial gain, and self-importance are all reasons why people seek supernatural experiences. But none of these are legitimate motives. The only legitimate motive for seeking spiritual experiences is a desire to grow in Christlikeness and love for others, where your desire is to bless them with what you experience. Let's not forget the Apostle Paul's admonition:

> *Though I speak with the tongues of men and of angels, but have not love, I have become sounding brass or a clanging cymbal. And though I have the gift of prophecy, and understand all mysteries and all knowledge, and though I have all faith, so that I could remove mountains, but have not love, I am nothing.*
> 1 COR 13:1-2

Before seeking supernatural experiences, you may want to take an inventory of your heart and examine the real reasons why you want them. Try not to rationalize that these experiences are okay because you *could* bless other people with them. If that is not presently your main desire, I would advise you not to seek further supernatural experiences until your heart has been transformed by the Holy Spirit. Supernatural experiences can draw you closer to God, but they can also provide an opportunity for Satan to increase his influence over you. The more supernatural experiences you have, the more likely you are to be motivated by wrong desires and the more likely Satan is to increase his influence in your life. A person whose heart has been made pure by the refiner's fire has little reason to worry about Satan gaining influence over them. These people are the best candidates to have their spiritual eyes opened further. They will take what the Lord reveals and use it not for themselves, but to bless others and to bring glory to God just as Jesus did.

Exercise

Throughout the book, you'll find an exercise at the end of each chapter. I'd like to begin by having you recite a slightly modified version of the Apostle Paul's prayer from the book of Ephesians:

> *"I ask that the God of our Lord Jesus Christ, the Father of glory, may give me the spirit of wisdom and revelation in the knowledge of Him, that the eyes of my understanding would be enlightened; that I may know what is the hope of His calling, what are the riches of the glory of His inheritance in the saints, and what is the exceeding greatness of His power toward me who believes, according to the working of His mighty power which He worked in Christ when He raised Him from the dead and seated Him at His right hand in the heavenly places, far above all principality and power and might and dominion, and every name that is named, not only in this age but also in that which is to come."*
> [ADAPTED FROM EPHESIANS 1:15-21]

Notes

Notes

Notes

CHAPTER FIVE

The Spiritual World

MOST OF US ARE AWARE that we are spirit beings, but the knowledge many of us have is an intellectual knowledge, and not an experiential one. That is to say, that most of us experience life primarily as physical beings and not as a spiritual ones. We must come to understand in a deeper way that we are—first and foremost—spirit beings. We have our existence as a spirit, which is a real, living being that exists in the spiritual world 24 hours a day. The spiritual world is the world that is eternal. It is the dwelling place of God, angels, demons, and other spirit beings, including our own human spirits.

The spiritual world is the eternal realm that created the physical world and we never stop interacting with that world once our spirit is created. Even though it may appear at times as if we "enter" and "leave" the spiritual world, our spirit never ceases to exist in, and interact with that realm. The existence of our spirit does not start and stop when we have spiritual encounters. This might seem like an obvious point, but many people behave as if this is what actually happens. We forget that our spirit is continually interacting with other spirits in the spiritual world, until we encounter a demon face-to-face, have a bizarre dream, or have some other spiritual experience. These encounters jar us into considering the realities of the spiritual world that we so quickly forget. The problem is that we have been conditioned to think that we are primarily physical beings that occasionally have spiritual encounters, rather than seeing ourselves as spiritual *and* physical beings that are continually having experiences in *both* worlds.

Just as our physical body perceives things happening in the physical world continually, our spirit perceives things happening in the spiritual world continually. Any spirit being can interact with any other spirit being at any time, and these interactions never cease, even though we are often unaware of them. And as I'll emphasize throughout the book, it is our awareness, or where our mind is focused, that deter-mines our perception of what is happening in both the physical and spiritual worlds.

Spiritual Senses

In the same way that the physical body has five different senses through which it can perceive the physical world, our spiritual body has similar senses that allow it to perceive the spiritual world. This book pertains to only one of those senses—the ability to see the spiritual world. But I don't want readers to think we can discount the importance of the other spiritual senses.

At times, the only way we can perceive the presence of a spiritual being is by the spiritual aroma it gives off. This is often the case when we're in the presence of a demon, but angels can also be detected by the aromas they emit. I sometimes sense the presence of angels only through the intense feelings of euphoria that are associated with the glory of heaven, which they carry. Many people experience intense feelings of oppression, hopelessness or despair when they visit certain cities. They've come to understand that these feelings are not internal, but external, and that they are related to the spiritual condition of a city. These feelings are intended to call them to intercession. When they pray or conduct spiritual warfare against the powers of darkness that are oppressing the city, the feelings subside. Sometimes the only indication that you're in the presence of an angel or demon is the sound you hear when it speaks. Much of what we can understand about the spiritual world comes through an intuitive type of "knowing." When we receive revelation in the form of thought impressions, there is often no other sensory input that accompanies these experiences. We see, feel, and smell nothing. We just somehow "know" we are in the presence of someone or we're given information that reveals something we need to know.

It's easy to think that if we have one spiritual sense that is highly developed, it is the only one we need. Some people even identify themselves by the spiritual sense they use most often, calling themselves "feelers" or "seers." I believe every human has the same access to all the spiritual senses, because our spiritual bodies are created with the same essential functions. Our uniqueness as spiritual beings is not because some people have access to senses that others do not. Our uniqueness results from the spiritual senses we choose to develop, and how we interpret and apply the revelation we receive through them. The well-equipped believer must develop *all* of their spiritual senses in order to gain a fuller understanding of what is happening in the spiritual world.

In order to help readers understand the nature of the spiritual world, it seems important to have some kind of blueprint by which we can better understand it. I've read many accounts and testimonies where people have described the spiritual universe. All the accounts I found lacked the kind of detail I was looking for, that is, until I found Peter Tan's book *The Spiritual World*.

Tan is a missionary who developed a habit of praying and fasting once a year every spring. In 2006, during the thirtieth year of his annual fasting, he was given a series of experiences that revealed the spiritual universe in the greatest detail imaginable. From these experiences he wrote a book. What impressed me about Tan's account of the spiritual world was not just the scope of the revelation he received, but the fact that many of the testimonies I'd read previously fit somewhat neatly into Tan's description of how the spiritual universe is constructed and how it functions. The sections that follow on the spiritual body, spiritual light, spiritual communication, and thought, contain excerpts from Tan's free book, which can be downloaded from his website. (For the sake of clarity I've paraphrased most of Tan's writings and supplemented some of them with my own observations.) Before we take a look at the spiritual world, I'd like to share an illustration:

In the classic sci-fi movie *The Matrix*, Keanu Reeves' character, Neo, suspects there's something wrong with the way life is being portrayed to the masses. He believes there is a world that is different from the one everyone sees—an invisible world that operates under a different set of realities—a world known as "the matrix." Neo does as much investigation as he can to learn the truth about what the matrix is and how it functions, but he never finds any solid proof to validate his suspicions. In a meeting with his new mentor, Morpheus, he's finally given a chance to see the workings of the matrix firsthand. Morpheus offers Neo two choices that come in the form of a pill. Morpheus tells Neo: "This is your last chance. After this, there is no turning back. You take the blue pill, the story ends, you wake up in your bed and believe whatever you want to believe. You take the red pill, you stay in Wonderland and I show you how deep the rabbit hole goes." Neo takes the red pill, is unplugged from the matrix, and wakes up in a world that is more bizarre yet more real than he ever imagined possible. Welcome to the spiritual world.

The Spiritual Body

The spiritual body is young in appearance. Those who see spiritual beings report that a person's spiritual body looks something like their physical body did in the prime of life. There is often a similarity in the facial features of a person's physical and spiritual bodies. There is a translucence to the spiritual body, but it also has a solidness and lightness to it that is derived from spiritual substance from which it is made. One of the chief differences between the physical and spiritual bodies is that the spiritual body emanates light. Not all spiritual bodies emit the same quality of light. Just as each physical body is unique in appearance, each spiritual body has its own unique qualities that differentiate it from others. The spiritual maturity of an individual can be discerned by observing the countenance and quality of light emitted from their spiritual body. A spiritual body is not always the same size as its physical counterpart. It has the ability to expand and contract to some degree, which is a result of spiritual growth.

Spiritual Light

The light of Christ which shines from His throne in heaven is the source of all light found in the spiritual world. Even the light of the brightest angel is merely a refraction of the light of Christ. This light is the source and sustainer of all life in every sphere of existence. The light of Christ is always present even though many spirits—particularly those in the lower spiritual realms—do not have the ability to appreciate His light. The reason why spirits of the lower realms cannot perceive this light is not because it is not present, but because their own spiritual blindness has prevented them from seeing it. Their spiritual eyes are not yet developed enough to see the light of Christ.

When we speak of the light that emanates from a spiritual body, we are not speaking of photons of visible light, but rather the spiritual light of heaven which gives life to all things spiritual. Photons of visible light only illuminate one side of an object and natural light casts a shadow. Spiritual light does not cast shadows. It penetrates and shines through objects in both the spiritual and the physical realms.

Spiritual Communication

When I speak to my wife, the sound she hears is the result of different forms of energy being transmitted through physical structures of the human body. My lungs exhale air through a set of vocal cords that stretch and contract to form sound waves, which are shaped by my mouth. The sound waves travel through the air and are picked up by her ear drum. The structures in her ear transmit the sound waves and change them into an electrical signal which is carried to her brain through the auditory nerve. Her brain processes the signal and converts it into the familiar voice of her husband. When she sees a flower, rays of light of different wave lengths pass through the lens in her eye and are projected onto the retina. From here, the waves of light are transferred to the optic nerve and sent to the brain as an electrical signal. The brain decodes and interprets the signal as that of a flower.

Spirit beings do not have physical structures like ear drums, vocal cords, retinas or optic nerves. When we see a demon or angel, we are not seeing them with the physical structures of our body. Their body does not emit waves of visible light that pass through the lens of our eye. When we hear a demon or an angel speak, the sound is not a wave that comes from their lungs that travels through our ear drum to the auditory nerve and then to our brain. Even though it *seems* as if we are hearing an audible voice like any other human voice, or seeing a physical body like any other body, spirits do not have physical bodies or the structures of communication required to create audible speech. Spiritual communication uses a completely different set of senses. Spiritual communication is done primarily through the transmission of thought impressions and visual imagery directly from spirit-to-spirit. It bypasses the physical structures of the human body. Allow me to illustrate what this looks like:

When an angel appeared in my bedroom one night to give my wife a message, she heard what sounded like an audible voice speaking, but I heard nothing, even though I was awake at the time. If the angel would have spoken in an audible voice, I would have heard the message, too. Audible messages are carried through sound waves and they can be heard by anyone nearby. But the angel didn't speak in an audible voice. It spoke directly to my wife's spirit, which is why she was the only one who heard the message.

When a demon speaks to the person sitting next to you in a restaurant, you can't hear what the demon is saying, but they can. This is because spirit beings have the ability to direct their messages to specific targets, while concealing them from those who are nearby. If spirit beings com-municated in ways that relied on the structures of the physical body, everyone nearby would hear them speaking just as clearly as the one they were speaking to. Spirit beings also have the ability to manifest their appearance to certain individuals, while remaining invisible to others. This is why some people see demons and angels manifest, while those nearby see nothing.

Thoughts

All spiritual beings emanate spiritual light through their thoughts. The light that is emanated reveals the various strengths and weaknesses of the spirit, the various areas of perfection, and the various areas of differentiation and characteristics. Light in the spirit world is like blood. In the physical world, life is in the blood (see Lev 17:11). In the spiritual world, life is in the light (see Jn 1:4). Because spiritual thoughts are composed of spiritual light and spiritual light originates in the glory of Christ, thoughts in the spiritual realm are quite powerful. Jesus said, *"And the glory which You gave Me I have given them, that they may be one just as We are one"* (see Jn 17:22). The glory given to the Son by the Father is the same glory the Son has given to us. This glory is the spiritual light that we receive into our spirits, which manifests as our spiritual thoughts. Because it has its origin in God, it has the same creative power.

When the Lord created the earth, it is easy to imagine that He spoke the earth into existence in the same way you or I would speak to a dog to tell it to sit. Yet we know that because God is a Spirit, He does not speak in the same way we speak. He does not force air from His lungs to create sound waves that travel through the air. His speech is a kind of spiritual thought, which emanates from Him. It carries creative power and it accomplishes His will. All creative works—including creative miracles—are done in the spiritual world through thoughts. (I'll discuss this concept more in chapter ten.)

All of our thoughts emanate light or darkness according to our inner spiritual life (see Matt 6:22, 23). The thoughts of those who live on earth can be seen in the spiritual world like a light that radiates from us in various colors. The light or darkness of our inner nature can be discerned by observing this light. This luminance flows from the character of our thoughts and can reveal all of our strengths and weaknesses. Through it, God and the angels are able to see what areas in our lives still need help and which areas need to be changed. When the Bible says that God looks at the heart, it is saying that He is literally able to see the kind of thoughts and intentions that are transmitted by our spirit, which are clearly visible in the spiritual world. In the same way, demons are able to see the spiritual light that we emanate—or lack thereof—and they can tell the areas of our lives that are under bondage to sin and weakness. No one can hide who they are in the spirit world; it is plain for all to see each person's character, strength, and weakness through the spiritual light they radiate (see Mk 4:22).

While the words that we speak usually flow from our spiritual thought life, it is possible for our spirit to communicate one thing, while our words speak something else. Sometimes our words are lies that intentionally mislead people about facts we are aware of in our spirit. Other times our words are merely the repetition of phrases we've learned to say in certain situations, but these words don't agree with our inner thoughts. We parrot them because we're afraid to say what we're thinking. If you've ever been in a situation where your mind was in a panic, but you were telling everyone around you to remain calm, this is what I'm referring to. The bible refers to this as being double-minded. It's a state where our words and our inner thought life are not in agreement. The apostle James warned that double-mindedness prevents us from receiving the answers to our prayers (see Jas 1:6-8). The reason is because God responds to faith, and double-mindedness leaves us living in fear, and unbelief, while insisting that we believe.

Double-mindedness is the reason why many times a demon will not leave when you tell it to— even when you command it emphatically to leave in the name of Jesus. We're accustomed to communicating with humans that have physical bodies that can hear our words. But demons don't have physical bodies and they cannot hear the actual words we speak. Instead, they receive the spiritual thoughts that are emitted from our spirit. (Remember, communication in the spirit world is done through the transmission of thoughts.) Demons respond to what our spirit is thinking and not to the actual words we say. For that reason it is just as easy to make a demon flee by thinking in your spirit that it must leave, as it is to tell it to leave with your mouth. This idea will seem odd to many of you so allow me to illustrate this point:

One of the most commonly encountered spirits is the paralyzing spirit, which often attacks people while they sleep. For this reason, its attacks are referred to as "sleep paralysis" by those who do not believe in demons. A common feature during these attacks is that the person is unable to speak. Yet it's often reported that these demons can be made to leave by thinking the name of Jesus or commanding the demon to leave in one's thoughts. No speech is needed to make them leave because they can't actually hear our words.

Many people have dreams in which they know things about others without being told. I've had many dreams where I knew what certain people were planning to do in advance. No one informed me of their plans. I simply knew with certainty their motives and their plans and the events played out in the dreams just as I knew they would. In my wife's dream where she met Jesus, He didn't walk up to her and say, "Hi, I'm Jesus." As soon as He appeared in the dream she knew who He was. How is it possible for us to know something about another person without anyone telling us? In the physical world, such knowing is impossible. If you want to know who someone is or what they plan to do, you must be told this information. But in the spiritual world, information is conveyed to others and assimilated by us through thoughts. This is true for demons, angels and all spirit beings.

You might be wondering why the Bible instructs us to speak against darkness, rather than think against it, if the real power is in what we think. While it's true that there can be great power in the words that we speak, this is only true when our words reflect our inner-most thoughts, and our inner-most thoughts are the things we believe in our spirit. Our spirit is where faith resides. And it is faith that God and the rest of the spiritual world recognize and respond to. If our words tell a demon to leave, while our spirit is transmitting thoughts of fear, the demon will perceive that we are afraid, and it will not leave. It is only when our words match the thoughts of our spirit—and we are single-minded—that the spirit world responds to what we say.

The thoughts of spirit beings that live in the heavenly realms can be detected by those who dwell on the earth. They radiate and inspire the thoughts of the people on the earth through the work of the Holy Spirit. The thoughts of evil spirits, who live in the spheres of darkness also influence and affect the thoughts of people on the earth who lean toward darkness. How much these thoughts influence humans depends on the inner strength and character of each human heart. Light attracts light and darkness attracts darkness. It is the free choice of all humans to decide which realm of thought influence they will yield to.

The effect of thoughts originating in the spiritual realm on the physical earth is greater than we realize. These effects, combined with the work of angels and saints which oppose the work of evil spirits, are the cause of all the activities that are seen on the physical earth. The invisible realm influences the physical world to an astonishingly great degree.

The Soul

Our spirit is what links us consciously to God and the rest of the spiritual world. Our body is what links us to the physical world, and our soul is the connector between the two. It is the meeting place and communication juncture between the physical and spiritual worlds. The soul gives us our conscious awareness of ourselves. It is able to perceive the spiritual world as easily as it perceives the physical one. Whichever world the soul is focused on at any point in time, that is the one we are most aware of, and it's the one we perceive to be the most real. Input from that world is received by the brain and acted upon, while input from the other world is largely ignored.

Most of us are bombarded continually by noise from the physical world, which drowns out the things that are going on in the spiritual world. Things like TV, radio, computers, and video games create a continual flow of information our mind must focus on and process. When our mind is asked to focus on these things repeatedly, it becomes biased toward things in the physical world and biased against things in the spiritual world. Since we're always having experiences in the spiritual world, even when we do not perceive them, the trick is to increase our soul's *awareness* of those experiences. One good way to become more aware of them is to tune in to the spiritual world, by tuning out the physical one. If you turn off sources of noise in the physical world and spend time quietly looking and listening for things going on the spiritual world, you'll be surprised at how accessible the spiritual world really is.

The human brain continually processes input from the physical senses of touch, taste, sight, smell, and sound. Because our brain is accustomed to processing information coming from the physical world, when information from the spiritual world is received, the brain may not know how to process or interpret it outside of the normal context of the physical world. Much of what goes on in the spiritual world is so different from what we experience in the physical world that we have little ability to make sense of it. The fantastic imagery and strange messages that come from the spiritual world can be so bizarre that they're often thought to come from our imagination. This is why messages from God, demons, and angels are often interpreted as our own thoughts. It is also why dreams remain a mystery to many people, even though they contain valuable information from God.

The brain must be re-conditioned to receive and interpret communication coming from the spiritual world. The apostle Paul contrasted the world's way of thinking with the heavenly way of thinking, reminding us not to have our thoughts conformed to the world's standards, but to have our life transformed by the continual renewing of our mind (see Rom 12:2). Learning to see and interpret things that come from the spiritual world is part of the process of renewing our mind. As we receive revelation from heaven and meditate on it, our patterns of thinking are changed and our behavior is conformed to the heavenly pattern.

If we truly are spirit beings that are created with spiritual eyes that can see in the spiritual world, then the problem with seeing in the spirit is not that we don't have the visual apparatus to do it, or that we lack the proper anointing or a spiritual gift. The problem is that our soul has not been conditioned to correctly perceive what our spiritual eyes are already able to see. Even people born with physical blindness have the ability to see perfectly in the spiritual world during near-death experiences.

When the physical body dies, the spirit and soul interact with other spirits and see things in the spirit world with ease. It is not as if at death, our spirit is suddenly empowered with abilities it never had before. It is simply that at the point when our physical body dies, its shell is removed, revealing the true nature of our spirit and soul as they always were. The spiritual body was always able to see in the spiritual world, and communicate with spiritual beings, but with the physical body out of the way, the soul can now focus more easily on the realities of the spiritual world. Every spiritual being has the ability to see in the spiritual world.

The Imagination

When we speak about our imagination, many of us think back to our childhood and the imaginary friends we had, the stories we made up, or the games we played to amuse ourselves. Children find it easy to engage the imaginary realm. As adults, we learn that society sees the imaginary realm as one of foolishness and make-believe. We're told that the only adults who engage the imaginary realm are hopeless daydreamers and the mentally ill. The phrase, "It's just your imagination," is used to dismiss the inspired ideas that come from this part of the soul.

In Genesis 8:21 the Lord said, *"I will never again curse the ground for man's sake, although the imagination of man's heart is evil from his youth."* In this verse, the Lord identifies the location of the imagination. It resides in the "heart" of man. The Hebrew word *leb*, translated "heart" does not refer to the physical heart, but the inner man, or what we commonly call the soul. Some people take this comment from God to mean that the human imagination in incapable of anything but evil. They believe we must resist any influence that comes from our imagination. But there is another way in which this verse can be interpreted.

The imagination can create things of beauty as well as things that are hideous. It is capable of creating both the sublime and the profane—that which is good and that which is evil. Because we have free will, we are capable of choosing what we create in our imagination. The passage in question simply states that prior to the flood, people chose to exercise their free will for evil purposes. They preferred to entertain evil in their imagination rather than good. Free will allows us to choose either one.

Man is made in the image of God, who describes Himself as a Creator. We are most like God the Creator when we're engaged in the act of creation ourselves. Because we are created in the image of God, we've been given similar creative abilities that serve His divine purposes. The imagination is the creative center of the soul. It's the place where original creative ideas are formed, and where creative inspiration is received from outside sources, such as angels and the Holy Spirit. God created our imagination as a way to communicate His detailed plans and purposes for us. His will can be revealed through the visions and dreams we receive in our imagination.

When the Lord gave Noah instructions for building an ark, it seems likely that He may have revealed the dimensions of the ark, the materials to be used, and the process of constructing it through Noah's imagination. When He gave Moses details about the construction of the tabernacle, He wanted it to be a replica of things in heaven. Since Moses had limited information to work with, it seems likely that God imparted the information he needed through his imagination. And when the artisans and craftsmen were asked to create ornamental items for the tabernacle, the details were probably given to them through their imaginations.

One problem that must be addressed is the fact that revelations from both heavenly and demonic beings are received the same way—through the imagination. In addition to the beautiful scenes we're shown from heaven, the imagination stores the grotesque, the perverted, and the frightening images we've been exposed to over our lives. It is constantly being bombarded by the kingdom of darkness with unpleasant images intended to harass, intimidate, and enslave us. God wants to reveal things to us through our imagination, and the enemy wants to prevent us from receiving them. The goal of the enemy is to so pollute the flow of revelation we receive through our imagination that we'll decide we don't want to see anything at all. Because the imagination is part of the soul, and the soul is controlled by our will, we can willingly choose to do whatever we want with our imagination. Because much of the imagery in this part of the mind is painful, in order to avoid the pain associated with these images, some people have exercised their free will and chosen to completely shut down the flow of revelation that comes through their imagination. In an attempt to safeguard their soul from the enemy's attacks, they have unknowingly blocked their ability to receive revelation from God. If these individuals were to exercise their free will and make the conscious choice to receive revelation again through their imagination, their "spiritual eyes" would again be opened and they would be able to see in the spirit. The solution is not to avoid receiving all of the imagery that comes through our imagination, but to learn how to filter it by sanctifying our imagination for God's purposes.

Trigger Alert:

If you suffer from a condition such as PTSD, Multiple Personality Disorder (MPD), or Dissociative Identity Disorder (DID), the following exercise may trigger unpleasant thoughts and may cause you to suffer an acute episode, which could be dangerous to you. Please consider having a trusted friend or counselor in the room that is willing to assist you, if you decide to do this exercise. You may skip this exercise if you do not want to risk triggering an acute episode.

Exercise

Some people have made inner vows to themselves saying that they will never again see things from the spiritual world. These vows have power and they often prevent the ones who made them from being able to see in the spirit. If you've ever made such a vow to yourself (or to anyone else) it's a good idea to renounce this vow and tell the Holy Spirit your desire to see in the spirit again.

For the person who is plagued with unpleasant images when they access their imagination, it may be a good idea to begin by healing the painful emotions and traumatic memories from the past. Receiving healing of painful emotions and memories can be a fairly straight-forward process that consists of three simple steps:

1. Identifying the painful emotion associated with a particular event

2. Asking Jesus to take the painful emotion from you

3. Asking Him to heal the wound in your soul caused by it

For many people, emotional healing really can be that simple. The main problem I've found is that people who are extremely rational by nature tend to ask a lot of "why" questions in the middle of the healing process, which can cause distractions and impede the healing process. While God may at some point reveal why a certain event happened to you, in the immediate setting of emotional healing, the more important question is *how* the event affected you. When you recall the event does it evoke emotions of anger or sadness? Do you feel shame, guilt or some other emotion? If you focus on the emotions you're feeling, and identify them one-by-one and allow Jesus to heal them, it's likely that you'll be able to access your imagination without the fear of painful memories getting in the way. I've received healing from emotional wounds from my own childhood. I'd like to share the process I've used since then to help people receive healing. (You might ask a trusted friend to help you with this exercise or you can do it yourself.)

One of the things Jesus purchased for us on the cross is healing of our painful emotions. The Bible says that Jesus has borne our griefs and carried our sorrows (Is 53:4). If He has borne them for us then we do not need to carry them any longer.

Healing painful emotions usually requires you to go back to events in your life where you can feel an emotion that is troubling you. Once you have accessed the memory of a particular event and you feel the emotion associated with it, ask Jesus to come to you. If the emotion you're feeling is sinful, confess it as a sin and ask Him to forgive you of it. Say that you believe the blood of Jesus has taken away the penalty and consequences of your sin.

Identify the emotion you're feeling. Tell Jesus you want the emotion removed from your soul. Ask Him to heal the wound in your soul caused by the emotion. Tell him you receive His healing.

An optional step that some people find helpful is to ask Jesus to give you something positive to replace the negative emotion that He is removing. If you ask Him to take away sadness, you might ask Him to give you joy. If you ask Him to take away anger, you might ask Him to give you peace. If the emotion is there because you believed a lie about that situation, ask Him to show you the truth about it.

When you are done with this, bring the memory of the painful event to your mind again. If the emotion was healed, you should not be able to feel it any longer, but there may be a different negative emotion that you can feel. Determine what negative emotion is strongest and do the same thing with it that you did with the first emotion. Tell Jesus you want the emotion removed from your soul. Ask Him to heal the wound in your soul caused by it and tell Him you receive His healing.

When you are done, bring the memory of the painful event to your mind again. Once more, try to determine if there are any negative emotions. If there are, repeat this process until you can bring the event to your memory and you feel no negative emotions. This process can be used on any memories that are associated with negative emotions.

Notes

Notes

CHAPTER SIX

Types of Visions

ONE OF THE MOST COMMON ways that God communicates to us is through visions. Visions from God are nothing more than images that are seen by our spirit and transmitted to our soul, so they can appear in our imagination. If you try to recall what you ate for breakfast this morning, you might see a brief picture in your mind of a plate of bacon. When your brain retrieves the image of your breakfast from its memory banks and displays it on the little TV screen in your mind, you are experiencing the same thing God does when He gives you a vision.

The apparatus for seeing visions from God is the same apparatus that displays any other visual information in your mind. While some people try to make visions seem mystical, there is less mystery about them than most people think. Having visions from God is supposed to be a very normal experience.

Although visions generally appear as images in our mind, some visions can have the appearance of being external to us. When a vision has the appearance of being external to us, it usually conveys the same kind of information as one that would appear as an internal scene in our mind. Visions can be seen with the eyes open or closed and the content will not be affected. However, most people find it easier, at first, to see visions with their eyes closed, since closing their eyes blocks out distracting background images in the physical world. Over time and with practice you may learn to see visions easily with your eyes open. It's really just a matter of learning to focus your mind on what you're seeing in the spiritual world and ignoring what you see in the physical one. The different types of visionary experiences people have are described in the New Testament by different Greek words. Next, we'll take a look at the different types of visual revelation people receive and I'll give examples of each.

The Greek word **apokalupsis** is a commonly used word in the New Testament that describes a type of vision. It literally means "disclosure," "appearing," or "manifestation." It refers to something hidden that is being revealed. This term denotes something that God is unveiling for our consideration for a specific purpose. It is used in the first verse of the book of Revelation:

The Revelation (apokalupsis) *of Jesus Christ, which God gave Him to show His servants—things which must shortly take place.*
REV 1:1

Here's an example of this kind of vision from my own life: In this vision, my wife and I were standing next to each other. We seemed to be near water, but I could not see the ground or anything else, except a large door that stood before us. As I looked at the door, it swung wide open. After this, we turned to our left and another large door appeared before us, which swung open. We turned again to our left and another large door appeared, which swung open. We turned one more time to the left, and a fourth door swung open. I interpreted the vision as a sign that God was opening many doors for us and giving us several different paths that we might follow. The vision seemed to indicate that it was ultimately our choice which path we would follow, but He wanted us to know that all of them would carry His blessing.

Enupnion and **onar** are Greek words for the dreams that we have when we sleep. Dreams are a form of visual revelation from God that our spirit receives while our body is sleeping. Because our soul can become preoccupied during the day time, God will often speak to us when our body and soul are at rest. Most people have dreams from God, but they're unaware that dreams are actually messages from Him. The book of Job teaches that God speaks to us through dreams:

> *For God may speak in one way, or in another, yet man does not perceive it. In a dream, in a vision of the night, when deep sleep falls upon men, while slumbering on their beds, then He opens the ears of men, and seals their instruction. In order to turn man from his deed, and conceal pride from man, He keeps back his soul from the pit, and his life from perishing by the sword.*
> JOB 33:14-18

God manifested Himself to Solomon in a dream. In their conversation, God told Solomon to ask for anything he wanted. Solomon asked for wisdom to rule over His people. In the dream, God gave Solomon wisdom greater than anyone who ever lived. He also received great honor, riches, and a promise of long life if he would be obedient. When Solomon awoke, he realized all these things happened while he was sleeping (see 1 Kgs. 3:5-15).

Although I had a span of about 25 years where I did not have any dreams at all, I've been having them regularly for several years and most of them are from God. He uses my dreams for many purposes. Some are warning dreams where He alerts me to dangers concerning my health, and provides solutions to the problems that He shows me. Some dreams are about people He wants me to help in ministry. Some of my dreams are prophetic, where I see events that will happen in the future. Some dreams reveal character issues that He wants to address, and many of my dreams are instructive, where He teaches me about His kingdom and how He sees me, personally.

Horama is a Greek word for vision that literally means "that which is seen." It refers to a spectacle, a sight divinely granted in an ecstasy (trance) in sleep, or in a vision while awake. An example is found in Acts 16:9-10:

And a vision (horama) *appeared to Paul in the night. A man of Macedonia stood and pleaded with him, saying, "Come over to Macedonia and help us." Now after he had seen the vision immediately we sought to go to Macedonia, concluding that the Lord had called us to preach the gospel to them.*

This type of vision can be about almost any subject you can think of. It's not uncommon for people to see visions like this that are a separate revelation, while they are having a dream. You might see an angel who gives you a message, you might see a demon that needs to be rebuked, or it may simply be a vision of a person who needs your help.

One night I was asleep and I was having a dream, when suddenly I was shown a separate scene in a vision. I saw a man and his family who were stranded with their car on a highway, in a snowstorm. I knew that they needed help, but I also knew that God was not going to send help until someone prayed for them. So I began praying and asked God to send them help. I was sleeping when I first saw this vision in my mind, but as I prayed I gradually woke up and my wife heard me praying. She asked, "Honey, who are you praying for?"

I was confused and didn't know what she was talking about at first, because I wasn't aware that she heard me praying. I said, "What do you mean who am I praying for?"

She replied, "I heard you praying for someone. Who were you praying for?"

Then it dawned on me that I must have been praying aloud and she heard me. "I saw this family stranded with their car in a snowstorm and I knew that God wasn't going to send help unless someone prayed for them. So I started praying, but I didn't know you could hear me." She joined me in prayer and we asked God to send help to the stranded family.

Sometimes God will give us visions and dreams to encourage us to intercede for others, but there are other reasons why we might see them. Many people have frightening encounters the first time they see in the spirit. This is often through an encounter with an evil spirit that attempts to frighten or seduce them. These encounters typically occur at night, when the person is alone, because most people are tired and less likely to put up the same kind of resistance they would during the day time. They may also happen during the first stages of sleep. Many people report seeing a pair of glowing eyes looking at them. It's common to feel a deep sense of fear or dread when these spirits are present. The best strategy for dealing with demons is to identify their agenda and resist it. Many times they simply want to cause you to feel fear. If you resist becoming fearful, you'll usually find that they'll stop harassing you.

Horasis is a Greek word that refers to the type of vision we have when our Spirit man looks through our physical eyes and our physical body is able to see what our spiritual eyes see. This may sound a bit confusing, but it is just a transfer of information from our spirit to our soul through our body. This type of vision is seen with the eyes open. For that reason it is often called an "open vision." It usually looks like two scenes that are superimposed over one another; one in the physical realm and the other in the spirit realm. It may also appear as a completely spiritual scene that replaces what you would normally see in the physical realm. Some people who see in the spirit this way describe it as something like seeing a scene through the windshield of a car, where you can see both a scene in the distance and the surface of the windshield with bugs and dirt on it at the same time.

One day while driving to work, I had one of these visions. Most of the visions I see are viewed with my eyes closed, but this one was different. I saw it with my eyes open. In the vision, I saw my EMT partner playing with a girl that appeared to be his daughter. (I didn't know for certain if she was his daughter as I had never met her or seen her picture.) I saw my partner kneeling down in front of her. She had blonde hair, and they were in a grassy area. There were other kids around them. I had a sense while looking at this scene that it had something to do with his future and it seemed to involve children. Then the vision suddenly changed and I saw him wearing a security guard uniform. (You might think it would be dangerous, but it was easy (for me) to concentrate on driving while seeing what was shown to me in the vision. Your experience may be different. It may be best *not* to operate dangerous machinery if you're having such an experience.)

When I got to work, I told my partner about the vision and what I thought it meant. I told him that if an opportunity came open to be more involved with kids he should consider it, and that if an opportunity came open to change careers and take a job as a security guard, he should not be afraid of leaving EMS. He confirmed the vision. His daughter, who was nine years old, had blonde hair. He showed me a picture of her and she looked like the girl I saw in the vision. It turned out that his new girlfriend, who lived in Oregon, had asked him to help coach soccer and baseball teams. He also said he was going to be moving to Oregon soon and a security guard position came open in the town he was moving to. He was planning on applying for the job after he moved there. One way in which God uses visions is to confirm His plans.

Optasia is a Greek word that literally means "visuality," or "apparition." It refers to seeing the manifestation of an individual person or being. Here is an example from the New Testament:

> *But also some women among us amazed us. When they were at the tomb early in the morning, and did not find His body, they came, saying that they had also seen a vision* (optasia) *of angels who said that He was alive.*
> LK 24:22

My friend Steve Harmon had been working with afriend who needed deliverance. They had been learning a lot about how to overcome the strategies used by demons. As Steve and his friend were about to leave for home, Jesus manifested His presence beside them and told them he was very proud of them and what they had accomplished. He said that the things they were doing and learning were the kinds of things no one else had yet considered or tried, and that their willingness to think outside the box and to resist the temptation to be afraid of trying new things was the key to all the amazing discoveries they had made.

In visions of this type, you might be visited by an angel of God, Jesus, or another heavenly being. They may comfort you or direct you to do something. Or you might be confronted or harassed by a demon. The point of these experiences is that God wishes us to be aware of the presence of other spirit beings.

Ekstasis (from which we get our English word ecstasy) is the Greek word most often translated "trance." It literally means "a displacement of the mind," or "bewilderment." Peter was given a vision from God concerning the Gentiles where God lowered a sheet with unclean animals on it. He saw this while he was in a trance (see Acts 10:9-17).

My friend Tom Calkins went into a trance for about five hours. One night as he was standing beside his wife in church, worshipping God, he suddenly felt the sensation of heat on his arm and he asked (in his mind) "Lord, is that you?" As soon as he did this, he was taken into the spirit world in a trance. While he was in the trance, he had a number of experiences with the Holy Spirit including a powerful revelation about the glory of God and the realities of speaking in tongues. While he was in the trance, his body was as stiff as a board and immovable. His wife and friends carried his rigid body out of the church and placed it in a van. They drove him to the pastor's house and placed him on a couch until the trance ended.

Egenomehn ehn pneumati is a Greek phrase that is literally translated "to become in the spirit." It is a state in which we see and interact with beings in the spiritual world and receive revelation directly from the Holy Spirit. It is, in a sense, being in a mental and spiritual state where our primary perceptions and actions have to do with things in the spiritual world and we are momentarily less aware of what is happening in the physical one. The Apostle John had several experiences of this type:

> *I was in the Spirit* (egenomehn ehn pneumati) *on the Lord's Day, and I heard behind me a loud voice like the sound of a trumpet, saying, "Write in a book what you see, and send it to the seven churches:*
> REV 1:10-11 NASB

> *After these things I looked, and behold, a door standing open in heaven, and the first voice which I had heard, like the sound of a trumpet speaking with me, said, "Come up here, and I will show you what must take place after these things." Immediately I was in the Spirit* (egenomehn ehn pneumati); *and behold, a throne was standing in heaven.*
> REV 4:1-2 NASB

One day my wife had an experience of this type. She had been asking God to show her things in the spiritual world for some time. One day, just after lying down to take a nap, she found that she couldn't sleep. Suddenly she became aware of the sound of a radio playing in our bedroom. (We don't have a radio in our room.) So she got up out of bed to find out where the sound was coming from. As she did this she became aware that she was still lying in bed while also being conscious of the fact that she was standing in the middle of the room. She was literally in two places at once, or at least that's how she perceived things. Next, she saw a ridiculous-looking demon standing in the hallway leading to our bedroom. The demon looked something like a crudely constructed fabric doll about 18 inches tall with sewn on eyes, nose, and mouth. She immediately sensed it was evil, but had no fear of it. The demon ran toward her and she knew she had to kill it. She grabbed it around the throat and strangled it. At this point, the part of her that was standing in the room came back into the bed. As her spirit and soul reunited with her body in the bed, she suddenly felt the full weight of her body in the bed again.

In this experience, she was literally translated into an event that was occurring in the spiritual world. This might be a little difficult to understand, but it can be seen this way: She became a primary participant of something happening in the spiritual world while her participation in the physical world was temporarily put on hold. After the experience was over, her primary experience was again based in the physical world. The experience provided several benefits to her: It made her more aware of the realities of the spiritual world and just how closely the spiritual world parallels the physical one. It also made her more aware of the presence of demons and it gave her a bit more determination to do battle against them.

Pursuing the Vision

The Bible is full of strange visual experiences. The visions shown to Ezekiel and Daniel portray the otherworldly realities of the spiritual universe. The experiences the Apostle John had concerning Jesus and the heavenly realms are some of the most important ones ever given to man. But the experiences of the prophets and apostles were not given exclusively to them. These saints and their experiences serve as examples for believers of all ages. The things they saw are possible for us to see. The things they did, we can do. Next, we'll examine the visionary experiences of Nebuchadnezzar and Daniel, which provide keys that can teach us how to pursue the visions God wants to show us. Several things are worth noting in the descriptions of their visions: First, notice how often the writers refer to images they saw in their mind. Second, consider how intentional they were about pursuing the visions to their completion. Let's take a look at some passages from the book of Daniel that illustrate these points. (I've highlighted parts of the text in bold for emphasis.)

> *I, Nebuchadnezzar, was at ease in my house and flourishing in my palace. I saw a dream and it made me fearful; and these fantasies as I lay on my bed and the **visions in my mind** kept alarming me.*
> DAN 4:4-5 NASB

> *Now these were the **visions in my mind** as I lay on my bed: I was looking, and behold, there was a tree in the midst of the earth and its height was great.*
> DAN 4:10 NASB

> *I was looking in the **visions in my mind** as I lie on my bed, and behold, an angelic watcher, a holy one, descended from heaven.*
> DAN 4:13 NASB

Next we'll look at the dreams and visions God gave Daniel. As with Nebuchadnezzar, the visions appeared in Daniel's mind:

> *In the first year of Belshazzar king of Babylon Daniel saw a dream and **visions in his mind** as he lay on his bed; then he wrote the dream down and related the following summary of it.*
> DAN 7:1 NASB

> *I was looking in my vision by night, and behold, the four winds of heaven were stirring up the great sea. And four great beasts were coming up from the sea, different from one another.*
> DAN 7:2 NASB

When the vision began, Daniel realized he needed to pay close attention to it. He focused his attention and "kept looking" into the vision as noted in the following three verses:

> *The first was like a lion and had the wings of an eagle.* ***I kept*** ***looking*** *until its wings were plucked, and it was lifted up from the ground and made to stand on two feet like a man;*
> DAN 7:4 NASB

> *After this,* ***I kept looking*** *and behold, another one, like a leopard...*
> DAN 7:6 NASB

> *After this* ***I kept looking*** *in the night visions, and behold, a fourth beast...*
> DAN 7:7 NASB

In the next verse, Daniel was contemplating the horns that he saw. As he thought about their meaning, the Lord showed him another horn:

> *While I was contemplating the horns, behold, another horn...*
> DAN 7:8 NASB

As we focus our attention on the revelation we are shown, God will often give us more information to further our understanding. As Daniel pursued the flow of revelation he was shown in the first vision, he was suddenly given a new vision of the throne of God the Father. It's not unusual for people to see heavenly scenes like these in visions and dreams. In the followwing scenes, part of the revelation petained to things happening on the earth, while another part pertained to things happening in heaven.

> ***I kept looking*** *until thrones were set up, and the Ancient of Days took His seat; His vesture was like white snow and the hair of His head like pure wool. His throne was ablaze with flames, its wheels were a burning fire.*
> DAN 7:9 NASB

Daniel continued looking into his vision and it became apparent that what he was seeing was a proceeding in the court of heaven:

A river of fire was flowing and coming out from before Him;
thousands upon thousands were attending Him, and myriads
*upon myriads were standing before Him; **the court sat**, and the*
books were opened.
DAN 7:10 NASB

Finally in verse 13, Daniel sees Jesus appear before the throne of the
Father:

I kept looking in the night visions, and behold, with the clouds of
heaven One like a Son of Man was coming, and He came up to
the Ancient of Days and was presented before Him.
DAN 7:13 NASB

I've had several nights where the Lord kept me up most of the night
showing me visions of different things. Sometimes I would feel tired
the next day, but occasionally, I would feel as if I had a full night of
sleep, as though God had given me supernatural rest. In these experiences I've found it important to pay close attention to the details that
are given, and to focus intently on what I'm seeing. As Daniel wrote,
it's important to keep looking for more revelation. It's an exercise of
our will to pursue the vision through to its end.

Spiritual Backgrounds

There are an almost infinite number of things you might see in the
spiritual world. Some of them are background objects that are always
present in a certain place. When my wife and I began doing nightly
"seeing" exercises at bedtime, we've noticed some things that were there
in our bedroom every night. (If you're not seeing in the spirit right now,
you might consider doing these exercises. They can be extremely helpful.
Information on the exercises will be included at the end of the chapter.)

My wife had never been able to see in the spirit with her eyes open,
but her desire was growing stronger. She purchased Michael Van Vly-
men's book *How to See in the Spirit* and we began doing some of the
exercises he recommended. One of the things that concerned her is
that Michael was able to spend a lot of time in prayer, which helped

him see in the spirit more effectively. My wife felt like she didn't have the kind of time needed to see in the spirit. Michael became a friend of ours and said that his wife also wanted to see in the spirit, but she didn't have as much time available as he did. He said that because of her great passion she developed her ability to see in the spirit in less time than it took him. Michael believes that desire is a key part of developing our ability to see in the spirit.

In the evenings, my wife and I lie in bed in the darkened room with a little bit of soft light filtering in through the window blinds. It's helpful to have a little bit of light present, but not too much. We relax ourselves on the bed and look at the empty space between us and the ceiling. When we first began doing these exercises, my wife saw a group of small, dark shapes appear that looked something like spinning fans. As we did these exercises repeatedly, she saw these same shapes night after night. She also saw something between our bed and the window that looked like smoke trails rising to the ceiling. Sometimes they appeared more like strands of seaweed than smoke trails. I saw them too. The strange thing about them was that when we waved our hand through them, they swirled in the direction our hand moved, like you would expect with a normal smoke trail in the physical world, though they were not visible in daylight. Over the course of several weeks we noticed that they were visible in our bedroom every night. One night my wife asked God what the smoke trails were. He replied, "Where there's smoke, there's fire."

One night, as I let my vision focus on the space between me and the ceiling, after just a few minutes, I suddenly saw the night sky come into view. It was almost as if the ceiling in the bedroom had been removed. As soon as I saw the stars, I mentioned them to my wife. She began looking for them and in a few minutes she saw them too. As I practiced these seeing exercises every night at bedtime, I could always see the stars, even if I saw nothing else. My wife benefited greatly from these exercises and she is now seeing visions regularly.

Once you begin seeing visions, there is virtually no limit to the types of environments you might see. I often see underwater backgrounds in the visions God gives me. Almost as common are scenes that look like I'm somewhere on a mountain. It's not uncommon to see backgrounds that appear to be deep in space where stars, planets, and nebula surround you. Many of the backgrounds I see have a distinctly heavenly appearance.

God gave me a dream one night where I visited an unusual house. In the dream, I was moving through a beautiful forest along a path. When I have dreams and visions of this type, my movement is very smooth and quick and it almost seems as though I'm floating. Going in a certain direction happens by thinking about where I want to go. As soon as I decide to go this way or that, I move in that direction effortlessly. As I was moving along the wooded path, I saw an ocean beach to my right with waves breaking along the shore. It was a very tranquil scene and there were no other people around. As I moved along the path, I suddenly took a turn to the left and entered a small house. I was immediately drawn to the way in which the house was constructed. It appeared to be made of the finest exotic woods. The workmanship that went into making the joints where one piece of wood met another was like nothing I had ever seen. The joints were virtually invisible. This is not something most people would notice, but I happen to be a woodworker and I appreciate fine craftsmanship. I took a brief tour around the small house and I was simply amazed at how comfortable it was. I glanced upward and noticed that the house did not have a roof, but a beautiful canopy of trees overhead that provided a serene backdrop. The trees appeared to be hundreds of feet tall and yet I could see each leaf on every branch in exquisite detail. I stood there dumbfounded for what seemed like 20 or 30 minutes, just taking in the beauty of the trees overhead. It's hard to express in words the beautiful colors that I saw in the leaves of the trees. This house was so comfortable I felt as though I could spend eternity there.

In my father's house there are many mansions. If it were not so I would have told you. I go to prepare a place for you.
(JN 14:2)

Write the Vision

Not long after I began having dreams and visions, God asked me to share some of them publicly. I was scared to death at what people might think of my prophetic writings, but I wanted to be obedient, so I took up the task of writing down the dreams and visions He gave me and interpreting them. The first step was to start journaling the revelation I received.

I keep a pile of note cards on my nightstand with several pens and a small flashlight. Whatever revelation God gives me at night, whether visions, dreams, angelic messages, or anything else, I try to write them down immediately. Notice I said "try." I don't always succeed in writing everything down immediately. Sometimes I'm just too tired or lazy to write a dream down. I have a friend who keeps her laptop computer on a stand at her bedside. When she has a dream or vision she enters it in a word processing document that she keeps open. Some people prefer to use digital voice recorders to keep a record that can be transferred to a computer and transcribed if needed. However it's done, it's important to find a way to create a permanent record of the revelation you receive. It only takes a few minutes for a fresh dream or night vision to fade into oblivion, never to be remembered again.

If I have any sort of unusual spiritual experience, it goes in my journal. I record any significant prophetic words I receive to remind me what God has declared about my destiny, my calling, my gifting, my assignments, people I should partner with, strategies for victory, or anything else that comes by way of prophetic revelation. When I have a small pile of note cards with dreams and visions written on them, I transfer the information to a word processing document on my computer. (I keep a backup copy stored on a flash drive in the event that my computer hard drive fails.) The word processing document creates a searchable database I can use to look up dreams or visions I've forgotten about. When someone asks if I remember having a dream about an earthquake in Washington for example, all I have to do is type the words "earthquake" or "Washington" in the search box of the document and the computer will find matches for me.

I review my spiritual journal regularly and ask God to help me interpret the dreams and visions I haven't fully understood. My friends find it amusing that I can accurately recall dreams I've had five years ago about them. What they don't know is that I consider my dreams to be one of the most important things in my life. I treasure them immensely and spend a lot of my free time meditating on the dreams and visions I've received. As I spend time reflecting on the revelation God has given me I always gain new insights into what He has been saying through them. I've learned that not every dream from God will come to pass in the way I expect. Here's one example:

I had been receiving dreams and visions about using revelation from God to help the police with unsolved murder cases. In the dreams and visions, I was given detailed information about the crimes, including street addresses and the locations of dead bodies. There were rewards available to anyone who could provide information that would lead to an arrest. I felt as though God had offered me an opportunity to help solve these crimes. I struggled for a while with fear that I was being disobedient to God by refusing to get involved in these cases. I wanted to be obedient, but there were personal reasons why we were reluctant to go through this door that God had opened. Not long after I made my decision not to get involved in these cases, the subject of my dreams changed. I no longer had dreams about murder cases. Most of my dreams turned to the subject of healing and prophecy, which I was very passionate about. As I embraced healing and prophecy with enthusiasm, the dreams and visions about those subjects increased.

The fact that God had opened a door for me that I was reluctant to go through may have been what He was illustrating in the vision with four open doors. There were different paths He would make available to me, but I didn't have to choose all of them. I never felt any condemnation from God about my decision not to help the police solve murder cases. The worry and guilt I did feel seemed to come from the enemy. Eventually, I learned more about God's plan for my life. I discovered that not everything He shows me carries the imperative that I must either obey it, or suffer the consequences of disobedience. Rather than handing me a "to do" list, like an angry step-father might, what He gave me was more like a menu, from which I could choose to do what I wanted, without feeling guilty over what I chose not to do. The dreams and visions of that season were laid to rest and I seldom think about them anymore. They had their time, and it passed. It's fruitless to fret over dreams and visions that pertain to a season that has passed. We must learn how to let them die and spend our time nurturing and cultivating the dreams and visions for the present season.

Exercise

Sit or lie down (whichever is more comfortable) in a darkened room that has a little bit of light present, but not much. The ambient light from a nearby streetlight may be enough light. If there are no outside lights nearby and the room is completely dark, you might use a small night-light to bring a little light into the room or consider turning on a light in another room and leave the door open just enough to allow a little light into the room. The first part of this exercise is to look at the empty space between you and the ceiling or a far wall for ten minutes. As you look, try to detect any images that appear either in your mind or in your field of vision and make note of them. Look to see if the images move or change shape and make note of what they do. The second part of the exercise is to ask God questions about what you see. Ask Him to interpret or explain the images you see and journal whatever you hear Him say. This exercise can be repeated as often as you'd like.

Notes

Notes

CHAPTER SEVEN

Angels

THE FIRST CHARISMATIC CHURCH I ever attended was a place where my wife and I learned a lot about the true life in the Spirit. Nevertheless, our pastor had a few beliefs he passed along to the congregation that quenched people's desire to learn about spiritual things, including his view of angels. We were studying the book of Revelation when he came to the passage where John fell to the floor and tried to worship an angel, who told him to knock it off (see Rev 22:8). I remember our pastor warning us in a stern voice: "We DONT worship angels!" That was the extent of what he taught us about angels. Sadly, many leaders today couldn't tell you much more than that. This is an unfortunate situation that must change if we're going to partner with God and reveal His kingdom to the world.

Angels are sent to us by God to assist us along our path of life. Depending on which source you read, angels are mentioned in scripture between 250 and 300 times. I don't intend to provide an exhaustive discussion on the subject of angels in this chapter. I simply want to give you a brief survey of how angels interact with humans and share a few testimonies. I hope to encourage you to learn how to cooperate with them to fulfill your own heavenly assignments and to help establish the will of God in your spheres of influence.

One of the most common ways that angels appear in the Bible is as messengers who impart instruction or news to people in dreams. In Genesis chapter 31, the angel of the Lord appeared to Jacob in a dream. The dream contained a symbolic message, which the angel interpreted. The message was that it was time for Jacob to return to his father's home. It's worth noting that this angel referred to himself as the Lord. It seems that this was a theophany, or an appearance of God in the form of an angel (see Gen 31:11-13).

When Abraham's servant was sent to find a wife for his son Isaac, an angel was sent with him to help prosper the servant during his journey (see Gen 24:40).

An angel gave Abraham's wife Hagar a message that her son, Ishmael, would not die of thirst in the wilderness, but that God had heard his cries and provided a pool of water for them (see Gen 21:17-19).

An angel shut the mouths of the lions and preserved Daniel's life throughout the night (see Dan 6:22).

An angel appeared to Manoah's wife to announce the birth of her child Samson. The angel gave her strict instructions about what to do in preparation for his birth. It was also revealed that her son would take the vow of a Nazarite, and that he would deliver his people from the Philistines (see Judges 13:2-5).

An angel appeared to Elijah after he called down fire from heaven to consume the armies of his enemies on two occasions. When a third captain approached and begged Elijah not to kill him, the angel told Elijah to go with the captain (see 2 Kng 1:15). When he was on the run from the wicked Jezebel, who wanted to kill him, an angel provided food and water for him in the wilderness (see 1 Kng19:5-8).

An angel appeared to Joseph, who was thinking about putting away his wife, Mary, when he found out she was pregnant. The angel appeared to him in a dream and instructed him not to put her away, because the child was divinely conceived. The angel told him what to name their child, and informed him that this child would be the Savior (see Matt 1:20-24).

The angel Gabriel appeared to Zacharias and informed him about the ministry of the child his wife was about to give birth to. When Zacharias doubted what Gabriel told him, the angel made him mute (see Lk 1:11-20).

An angel appeared to Cornelius and gave him instructions about how to find the apostle Peter, who would eventually come to his home and preach the gospel to the Gentiles for the first time (see Acts 10:1-7).

An angel stirred the water at the pool of Bethesda and brought healing to the first person who entered the water (see Jn 5:4).

After Herod had put to death James, the brother of John, and saw that the Jews approved of it, he had Peter put in prison and planned to bring him before the Jews after Passover. While Peter was in chains, an angel of the Lord came into the prison and woke him, saying that he should get dressed and follow him. The angel went before Peter and opened the prison gates then disappeared (see Acts 12:11, also see Acts 5:17-20).

An angel offered encouragement to the apostle Paul in the midst of a disaster at sea, telling him that all those who sailed with him would not perish in the storm, but that the ship would run aground and they be saved from death (see Acts 27:23-24).

According to the writer of the book of Hebrews, angels have been sent for the express purpose of ministering to those who will inherit salvation (see Heb 1:14).

The most common way angels have interacted with me and my wife is by delivering messages in the middle of the night. These messages usually come in the form of a voice that we hear speaking, sometimes in the middle of a dream or vision, but sometimes without reference to either one. The messages are usually short. They can have an obvious meaning or they may be somewhat cryptic. My wife received a message one night from a voice in the middle of the night that told her: "Beware of those who are called, but not chosen."

The Lord appeared to me one night to deliver a message about a revival that was about to happen where I lived. I heard His voice as clearly as any voice I'd ever heard, but I saw no visible manifestation of Him. I may have thought it was simply another angel delivering a message in the middle of the night, were it not for the fact that twice during the message he said, "I, the Lord..." When an angel identifies himself as the Lord, there is greater importance to the message.

One night I received nine visions together with one message that was only a voice speaking to me. I felt the presence of an angel in the room as the voice spoke, but I saw nothing. The voice said: "David McLain had a long interview with God last night and in that interview God asked him to step down from his position." My wife later had a dream where McLain resigned from his position at his church because he had "too many irons in the fire." Sometime later I had a chat with him about the messages we received. He took them as confirmation about the decision he had already felt led to make about stepping down from his position in the church.

My first encounter with seeing angels happened after a long day of demonstrating healing and deliverance. I was resting on the couch in my hotel room. I had received a few prayer requests by email and I was praying for one person to be healed. As I lay there on the couch with my eyes closed, I suddenly saw in my mind's eye four beings of light standing in a circle looking down at me. They had the strangest looks on their faces. They seemed to be amused by me. One of them had what looked like an enormous tree trunk in his hands and he appeared to be smashing something with it. I'm not certain, but I believe he was smashing a demon. The look of joy on his face was priceless.

One approach to healing and deliverance that is often overlooked is to recruit angels to help you. Angels hate demons. (Hate may actually be too soft a word to describe how they feel.) A few years ago I began dispatching angels to minister to people who sent me prayer requests by email. I didn't do this every time at first. I only did it once in a while, as I was led by the Holy Spirit. But it wasn't long before I began to use this approach routinely. As I would pray for someone with my eyes closed, I saw beings of light moving to and fro in the spiritual realm. Today, I nearly always dispatch angels of healing or deliverance when I'm praying for someone over a great distance. I know that there are angels who specialize in healing and deliverance and I believe they are waiting for us to send them out into the world to do the will of God with regard to healing the sick and setting people free of demonic oppression.

Healing angels have been seen carrying containers of oil that has the power to heal when it's applied to sick people. They have other ways of releasing healing as well. Angels can use their superior power on demons and cause them to feel discomfort and torment. There's nothing wrong with asking an angel to apply a little pressure on a demon that is resisting your attempts to make it leave. Demons often leave when confronted by a company of angels that intend to do them harm. I realize it may sound cruel to ask an angel to torment a demon, but to them it's just another assignment they must carry out in their roles as servants of men and God.

One day I had a conversation with Steve Harmon about a tricky deliverance he did with the help of some angels. Steve had been working for months on getting several people free from their demons. At one point he became terribly frustrated and asked one of the angels why they couldn't just tell him the information he needed to get rid of the demons. The angel said (I'm paraphrasing): "Steve, there's a reason why we don't make things easy for you. You need to grow and learn. If we always give you the answers without allowing you to go through the process of learning and finding the answers for yourself, you will never grow."

God's desire is that we would grow in knowledge and wisdom into the fullness of the stature of Christ (see Eph. 4:13). That is His plan for all of us. The kingdom of God is all about growth. God is more interested in our growth than anything else, including the healing of our headache or our deliverance from an evil spirit. Please note: I did not say that these things aren't important to God. They *are* important to Him. But in eternity, the importance of our spiritual growth far outweighs our temporary afflictions (see 2 Cor. 4:17).

Learning the keys to releasing healing requires us to ask the Holy Spirit for guidance. Asking Him for guidance requires us to become more familiar with His ways. Learning the secrets of operating in healing and deliverance requires us to mature in discerning the presence of spirits and how to deal with them. God doesn't make things difficult for us merely to cause us frustration. Difficulties are designed to force us to seek a greater understanding of God's nature and His kingdom. Every difficulty we encounter is intended to lead us to Him for the answer. Some of the answers are revealed when we learn how to better see the realities of the spiritual world.

Steve shared the following story about the time his angels manifested at a dance club:

"A couple of years ago I went to meet a friend for her birthday at a dance club. Let's call her 'Sarah.' I wanted to stop in and wish her a happy birthday. The moment I stepped on the property where the club was located I felt the Lord tell me 'spiritual warfare.' When I got inside the club it was packed with people, and I went looking for Sarah. I found and approached her, gave her a hug and told her 'Happy Birthday.' It was too loud to really carry on a conversation. So after that I went outside, talked to a few of our mutual friends and left. The next day she asked another friend of mine, 'Who were those two guys with Steve? Can you hook me up with one of them?'

She said back to Sarah, 'There was nobody with Steve.'

Sarah responded, 'Yes there was! There were two huge guys with Steve!'

The other girl responded, 'No, there wasn't.'

Then Sarah froze and started to freak out. She described what she saw. She said that she saw two huge guys, both around seven feet tall. They had big muscles, were well-built, had blonde hair, blue eyes and they were twins. They were wearing black suits, like secret service agents, and were both standing behind me. It's funny because Sarah is really attracted to guys with that appearance and she's not even five feet tall herself.

Well, I called her up the next day and she told me all about it. She wanted to know why she could see them. I told her that it was because God wanted her to know there is a spirit realm and that it is very real. I said to her that she now has a decision to make whether to follow Jesus or not because of what she saw. She chose to accept Jesus. God used the encounter with my angels as a sign to her. As time went on He started showing her other supernatural things.

Signs are not meant to be worshipped; they point to something. When you see a sign on the street that says 'turn right to go to Los Angeles,' you don't get out of your car and worship the sign on the street. You turn right to go to Los Angeles. The sign of seeing those angels pointed my friend to Jesus. It's precisely why we want to perform signs and wonders. We want to point people to Jesus."

Exercise

Choose a scene from the Bible where an angel appeared. Ask the Holy Spirit to show you what this scene looked like. Write in a journal what you see and anything that you hear.

Suggested verses:

Gen 21:17-19, Gen 31:11-13

Jud 6:11-23; Jud 13:2-23

1 Kng 19:5-8

Dan 6:22

Matt 1:20-24; Matt 4:11

Lk 1:11-20

Jn 5:4

Acts 5:17-20, Acts 10:1-7, Acts 27:23-24

Rev Chapter 5

Notes

Notes

CHAPTER EIGHT

Interpretation and Confirmation

IT'S UNDERSTANDABLE TO BE EXCITED about seeing visions and having dreams from God, but if you don't understand what they mean, it can be a very frustrating experience. It's critically important to be able to assign meaning to the revelation we receive. A common problem people have is discerning when a dream or vision is to be taken symbolically (as a parable) and when it is to be taken literally. As a general rule, if a dream or vision can be taken literally, it should be. However, if there is something in the dream or vision that is not literal, it is likely that the entire thing should be interpreted symbolically.

For example, if you previously owned a red sedan of a certain make and model and you dream that you are driving that car to a house you once lived in, the dream is probably speaking about an issue from your past. It's likely that the time frame of the event God is addressing is the time during which you owned that car. This dream should be interpreted symbolically, because the car you're driving in the dream isn't the actual car you own and the house is not the one you currently live in.

If, on the other hand, you dream that you are driving the car you presently own to the job you presently have, and in the dream you're involved in an accident on the street you actually drive to work, you should probably take this dream literally and drive carefully.

I once had a dream that I was driving a green Honda sedan that I owned at the time I had the dream. As I was driving, the temperature gauge indicated that the car was overheating. A few days later the timing belt on my Honda broke and the water pump failed, which caused the car to overheat. This was a warning dream intended to nudge me into having the car repaired. This is a classic example of a dream that is intended to be taken literally.

In his book *Understanding the Dreams you Dream*, Ira Milligan explains it this way:

> "There will normally be a key—a clue—something in each dream that will reveal whether it is literal or symbolic. As a rule, if there is an object or person in the dream that cannot be taken literally, then the entire dream should be viewed as symbolic or as a parable. However, if everything in a dream is as it is in real life, the dream is usually literal.
>
> For instance, I once dreamed that that my brother called me and asked if I was interested in renting a house that his employer had for rent. I said that I was, and in the dream I went and examined the house. It was a light-colored brick. Inside, the floor was littered with trash. I noticed that quite a lot of money was scattered among the trash.
>
> After I awoke, I was still meditating on the dream when my phone rang. It was my brother calling. He asked me the same question he had asked in the dream, 'Are you interested in renting a different house?' I replied, 'Yes, I've been praying for a better place.' When I actually saw the house it was identical to the one in the dream, trash and all. I rented it and in addition to the money that was

scattered on the floor, the landlord gave us half the first month's rent for cleaning it."

There will be occasional exceptions to the rules of interpretation, but most of the time, if there is something that is not to be taken literally in a dream or vision, it is likely that the entire dream or vision should be taken symbolically.

As tempting as it might be to take guesses at what a dream or vision might mean, the best method is to let God provide the interpretation. When the Lord first commissioned Jeremiah as a prophet, He had to provide some instruction in order to help him understand the visions he would see. We see his training played out in the first chapter of the book of Jeremiah:

> *The word of the Lord came to me saying, "What do you see, Jeremiah? "And I said, "I see a rod of an almond tree." Then the Lord said to me, "You have seen well, for I am watching over my word to perform it.*
> JER. 1:11-12

In the first vision Jeremiah was shown, he saw the branch of an almond tree and the Lord confirmed that he had seen correctly. The Lord then showed him another vision and asked what he saw. Jeremiah replied that he saw a boiling kettle facing north. If God were to have shown you this vision how would you have known what it meant? Jeremiah needed God to give him the interpretation. When Jeremiah answered correctly about what he had seen, the Lord told him what it meant: An army would come from the north to attack Judah and Jerusalem.

God did something similar with me when He began giving me dreams and visions. On the first night that I began having dreams and visions, I saw a scene reminiscent of Jeremiah's commissioning. I realized that God was going to give me visions and confirm that I was seeing and interpreting them correctly. In the first vision, I saw two pictures from an anatomy text book. One image was of a healthy liver and the other was a diseased liver. As I looked at the images, the anatomy textbook vanished, but the images remained. God asked me to tell Him what I saw. I told Him I saw a healthy liver and a diseased one, which looked like it had cirrhosis. He replied, "Yes." Then I saw a healthy stomach and esophagus, and a stomach with an esophagus that looked like it had esophageal varices from long term-alcohol use. I told Him what I saw and He said, "Yes." Next, I saw a healthy brain and one that appeared to have a tumor. I told Him what I saw and He said, "Yes." Then He said, "I want you to pray with your patients. I will show you what is wrong with them and when you pray I will heal them."

In this series of visions God tested my ability to see correctly, He confirmed that I had interpreted the visions properly and commissioned me to use my ability to see visions for healing. (God's purpose for you will be different than His purpose for me.) After this experience was over, I found a tablet of paper and a pen and wrote down what I saw and what God told me. I went back to bed, but before I could go back to sleep, He gave me another series of visions.

In the first vision, I saw a man that I had transported earlier in the day that I prayed with. He was a heroin addict. I saw him lying in a bed and noticed that his eyes were clouded over. He appeared to be sad, depressed and lonely. Next, I saw the light around him grow dim, then a brighter light appeared and finally he was visited by an angel. I had prayed for divine protection for him earlier in the day. I believe this vision showed how God answered my prayer.

Next, I saw myself placing my hands on various patients in a hospital. I was praying for them and prophesying to them. I did the same for the employees of the hospital. Some of the people I prayed with were in hallways; some were in patient rooms, and some were outside the hospital sitting on the sidewalk. This series of visions revealed that my ministry would involve praying for people as I worked in health care. Here are some of the visions God gave me over the next few months along with how I interpreted them:

In a night vision, my wife and I were encouraging someone to press through a present situation. We were encouraging him to be patient in waiting for God's timing. We told him to go into a room and close the door. Next, we told him to pray and remain in the room until God did what he needed to do, even if it took months. In this vision, God was showing me that my wife and I would be used to encourage people.

He was also emphasizing the need to patiently wait for His timing on certain things.

In the next vision, my wife and I were sitting with a friend. We were helping him sense the presence of God and we were praying and waiting for God's revelation to come. Here, God revealed that one of my main callings would be to help people sense His presence. He also emphasized the fact that sometimes we must wait for the revelation of His plan.

One night I saw a vision of Dutch Sheets and Chuck Pierce. For the benefit of those who don't know them, Dutch is an apostle and Chuck is a prophet. They've had a very successful ministry that's largely a result of their willingness to work together as partners. In the vision, Dutch was speaking. He said, "When I'm partnered with this man (pointing to Chuck) I prophesy more." After this vision I saw myself with a friend. I was getting to know him better and we were sharing our spiritual journey. It seemed like we were accountability partners. It also seemed that God wanted us to be aligned in a partnership to increase the effectiveness of our ministries, following the example of Dutch and Chuck.

In one vision, I saw myself in a large room. Although I've never been there, I somehow knew I was at the annual prophetic conference in Albany, Oregon. The prophetess Stacy Campbell was looking at me intently and getting a revelation from God about me. As she walked slowly around me in a circle, she suddenly said, "You have the gift! Are you using it?" In this vision, God was emphasizing the fact that I need to use the prophetic gifts He has given me.

One night I saw a vision of a nurse that I knew from work. I heard a demonic voice tell me "She likes to party, and her husband wants to stay at home and settle down." I asked, "Lord, is this true?" The voice (now sounding more hideous) said the same thing again. Again I asked, "Lord is this true?" The hideous voice began screaming about how the nurse partied and lived a wild life, and her husband didn't want her to live that way. I asked again, "Lord, is this true?" I heard a noble sounding voice say, "I want to heal her." In this vision, God confirmed that part of my calling was to partner with Him in healing. He also revealed the fact that the enemy likes to slander the people He wants me to minister to, and lastly, that He is willing to heal people in spite of what may (or may not) be going on in their personal lives. In each of these visions, once they were interpreted, God revealed some part of His plan to me. In the vision where the demonic voice was speaking about the nurse, I had to repeatedly ask God for more revelation.

We can see accurately the messages that God wants us to see, but if we're not careful, we can misinterpret or misapply what we've seen. The way in which we interpret revelation is determined by our view of God. There are many different views of God, even among Christians who might attend the same church congregation. This is one reason why there are so many conflicting opinions about what a particular dream or vision might mean. For several years I've been posting dreams and visions sent to me by friends on social media as public exercises to help people learn how to interpret them. It never surprises me when I see a wide range of interpretations revealing some very diverse (and sometimes frightening) ideas about how God views His creation. Among the people I know, the views of God can be roughly divided into two main categories: One view is primarily influenced by the writers of the Old Testament. People who hold this view of God tend to see Him as an angry deity who is generally displeased with mankind because of our failure to live up to His standards. They tend to interpret imagery of things like earthquakes, floods, or volcanoes as literal events depicting God's impending wrath upon mankind, because of our continued failures.

The other group tends to see God as a kind and benevolent Father who is extremely patient and understanding. They see Him as an encourager, a protector, a generous financier, a wise old sage, and a passionate lover, who seems to be amazingly proud of everything we accomplish, in spite of our failures. This group would tend to interpret visions of volcanoes and earthquakes as being symbolic of personal changes in the life of the ones who see them.

Until we rightly understand the heart of God, we cannot accurately interpret His messages. It's my personal opinion that much of what passes today as prophetic revelation from heaven is of very poor quality, not because people aren't able to receive revelation accurately, but because they have a distorted view of God. The distorted views come primarily from failing to interpret the Old Testament in light of the revelation of Jesus as the perfect image of God as He is portrayed in the New Testament. The best way to discover the true heart of God is to study the life of Jesus and develop a greater understanding of His ways through personal interactions with Him. That comes by spending a lot of time conversing with Him, asking questions, receiving answers and getting to know His heart. When we know the issues of His heart, we can more easily understand the meaning of the messages He gives us.

Is It God or Is It Me?

One of the most common questions I've been asked about receiving revelation from God is: "How do I know if a message I've received is from God, from my soul, or from the enemy?" For the purposes of this discussion, it might be easier to separate revelation into two types: that which is internal (that which comes from us) and that which is external (that which comes from a being that is outside of us.) It's not difficult to determine whether something you see or hear is from an internal or external source as long as you keep in mind a couple of key principles:

Imagine for a moment that you are the radio operator on board a ship at sea. Now imagine that your ship needs to communicate with another ship at sea. Communication between two ships is done by sending radio signals back and forth. As the radio operator on one ship, you might wonder how you can distinguish between the signals you are sending and the signals being sent by the other ship. Consider this fact: As the radio operator on your ship you're able to control the content of the messages you send, but you cannot control the messages coming from the other ship. The fact that you cannot change a message coming from the other ship means that the message had its origin somewhere else. The fact that you can change a message coming from your own ship means that it had its origin on your ship. This same principle applies to messages from God, angels, demons, and our own soul.

Our soul creates its own messages, including thoughts and visual images. One difference in visions that come from an external source and visions that come from our soul is that images that come from an external source are difficult or impossible to manipulate or change willfully. Just like the radio message sent by another ship, a message that is external to us cannot be changed by us. Whereas messages that originate in our soul can be changed by exerting our will over them.

A second principle to consider is that a message we might send to another ship requires our input. We must think of what we want to say and initiate the message willfully. Messages we receive from another ship are received spontaneously, with no effort on our part. Images and messages we receive from external sources tend to appear spontaneously with no effort on our part or involvement of our will, whereas images originating in our soul require some intention on our part (we must exercise our will) to make them appear or disappear.

Not all of the visions we receive from an external source are from God. Demons and angels can also send us visual images. The content of a vision is usually a reliable indicator of where it came from. Images of heavenly scenes and messages that convey hope, impart peace, joy, love or other qualities that are consistent with the nature of God are generally from Him. Images portraying spiritual darkness, depravity, perversion and sin, or visions that create intense feelings of hatred, fear, shame or guilt are usually (though not always) from the enemy.

There are times when God will show us things from the kingdom of darkness, and when demons will show us things that appear to be heavenly. How do we know if a dark image is from God or the enemy? The enemy shows us the things of darkness in order to draw us into them as a participant, while God reveals darkness to help us defeat it. When I sense that a vision is attempting to lure me into something evil, I know it is from the enemy. When I sense that the purpose of a vision portraying darkness is to highlight some problem that must be dealt with or overcome, I know it's from God. God has a redemptive purpose in all that He does, and you should be cautious when receiving revelation that doesn't appear to have a divine purpose. (Cautious, but not fearful.)

The confirmation that you're interpreting the things you receive accurately comes by examining the fruit produced by the experience. If you see a vision of a demon that causes you to experience feelings of fear, it is likely that you're seeing a vision sent by the enemy. If you reject this vision and resist the fear and the vision dissipates, you have confirmation that it was from the enemy. If you receive a visual impression that a stranger has back pain and you ask them about it and they confirm that they do in fact have back pain, the revelation is confirmed. You're seeing correctly. If you pray with them and they're healed, you have more confirmation that the vision was from God. If you sense the manifest presence of God as a tingling sensation on your skin and—by faith, enter into a time of worship that brings emotional healing—you have confirmation that you were sensing God's presence accurately. We know that we're interpreting and applying revelation correctly when we act on it in faith and the fruit of the Spirit is produced in our lives.

At first, the learning process can be a little frustrating but with practice you'll be able to quickly and confidently discern where visions come from, what they mean and how they're applied. Many of the symbolic images you're likely to see can be found in the Bible, and in some cases the meanings are provided. I suggest using the scriptures as an interpretation guide for symbolic images, until you develop a working spiritual vocabulary. Paula Price's book *The Prophet's Dictionary* is an excellent resource for identifying the significance and meaning of the most common things you're likely to see. Another excellent book is *The Divinity Code to Understanding Your Dreams and Visions*, by Adam Thompson and Adrian Beale, which has an extensive dictionary of images and their meanings.

I'd like to close this chapter with a story about an encounter we had with a friend that illustrates how God will confirm the things He shows you. My wife and I met with a friend named Sandy for coffee and prayer. Her sister had been diagnosed with Lou Gehrig's disease so we agreed to meet with her to pray for her sister to be healed. That morning as we prayed, I had my eyes closed and saw many different images of sunflowers. Some of the images looked like photographs while others looked like paintings. I had no idea why God would show me sunflowers, so I asked, "Is anyone else seeing anything, because all I'm seeing is sunflowers… lots and lots of sunflowers. Does that mean anything to anyone?"

Sandy said, "That's really odd. My daughter Candace loves sunflowers. Everything in her house has sunflowers on it. Her daughter wears shirts with sunflowers on them. Maybe it has to do with her." Sandy told us she had to get to a dental appointment and we had things to do at home so we said goodbye and drove home. Before we got home, we received a text message from Sandy asking us to pray for her daughter Candace. She was in her second trimester of pregnancy and she began bleeding so she went to the hospital. Sandy cancelled her dental appointment and went to the hospital to be with her daughter. When we got home we prayed for Candace and her baby. Later, Sandy sent us a message saying that the doctor had to do an emergency procedure to stop the bleeding and save the baby's life.

Before Sandy received the call about her daughter, God told her something was happening through the sunflower vision that He gave me. When God shows me something I don't understand, I've learned that if I share it with others, it will usually have a very personal meaning to someone.

Exercise

Spend fifteen minutes today in a quiet place where there are no distracting noises. Sit or lie quietly with your eyes closed, and ask God to show you one vision of something He wants you to see. Be still and let your heart focus only on Him. Whatever image you see in your mind no matter how faint it is, or how odd it might seem, ask Him what it means and wait for the answer. You might see another image, or a word or you might hear a thought impression. Write in a journal what you saw and what you believe He told you about it. You can repeat this exercise as often as you want.

Notes

Notes

CHAPTER NINE

Seeing in the Spirit and Prophecy

ONE OF THE MOST POWERFUL uses of our ability to see in the spirit is the gift of prophecy. An accurate prophetic word can bring hope to the despairing, and shed light on the dark paths that we sometimes travel. The apostle Paul instructed the church at Corinth:

> *Pursue love, yet desire earnestly spiritual gifts, but especially that you may prophesy.*
> 1 COR 14:1 NASB

There is a curious thing about the way in which God gives spiritual gifts to man. When you survey the New Testament for spiritual gifts, you may notice that they fall into three categories. One category contains the gifts that are given by the Father, one contains the gifts that are given by the Son, and one the gifts given by the Holy Spirit. The Father's gifts are found in Romans chapter 12, the Son's are found in Ephesians 4:11, and the gifts of the Spirit are found in first Corinthians 12. Only one gift is given by all three, and that is the gift of prophecy.

The gifts of Jesus are specifically given to the body of Christ—to those who believe in Him. These gifts are essentially positions of leadership. The gifts of the Holy Spirit that are found in first Corinthians 12 are gifts which are given to the church at large for the building up of the body of Christ. It has been suggested that the gifts of the Father are gifts that are given to all of mankind—Christian and non -Christian alike. These gifts can be thought of as the natural bent of a person's character. They can be used however one chooses—for good or for evil—or they can be completely ignored. I believe this is why some people who are not filled with the Holy Spirit can receive prophetic revelation with incredible accuracy. God the Father has given them the gift and they have chosen to exercise it. These people often make use of their gifts by operating as New Age gurus, shamans, psychics, Tarot card readers and energy healers. They learn how to operate in their God-given gifts, even though the source of their power and revelation may not be God himself. When they become filled with the Holy Spirit, their gifts can be very powerful. Ephesians chapter four reveals the gifts that Christ gave to the church:

> *But to each one of us grace was given according to the measure of Christ's gift...And He Himself gave some to be apostles, some prophets, some evangelists, and some pastors and teachers, for the equipping of the saints for the work of ministry...*
> EPH 4:7,11

While it's clear that some believers are called as prophets to the church, it is also clear that anyone can operate in the gift of prophecy. Paul wrote:

> *For you can all prophesy one by one, that all may learn and all may be encouraged.*
> 1 COR. 14:31

Whether you are a believer who prophesies to friends or a prophet with a sphere of influence to a nation, the process of translating visual images into a cohesive statement revealing the heart of God is the same.

Personal Prophecy

When we operate in prophecy as a gift of the Holy Spirit, our words are intended to bring comfort and encouragement to the body of Christ. This is the express purpose for all of the gifts of the Holy Spirit.

But he who prophesies speaks edification and exhortation and comfort to men...he who prophesies edifies the church.
1 COR. 14:3-4

For almost two years I've hosted a free prophetic word thread on a social network where anyone desiring to receive a word from God could leave a request for one. The thread collected over 18,000 comments. The prophetic words given have imparted hope, encouragement, and at times, direction for those who receive them. It also served as a training ground for people who want to learn how to prophesy in a safe environment. One problem we encountered was that for every six or seven people who requested a prophetic word there was only one person willing to prophesy. This mismatch leaves many people seeking a word, with no one to give them one. Because there is no lack of people who desire to receive prophetic words, I would encourage all believers to learn how to prophesy. If believers were more active in the gift of prophecy, people might be less inclined to seek advice from psychics and fortune tellers.

The gift of prophecy may require us to develop our ability to see in the spirit before it will function properly. God can send us messages for others in the form of visions, but if we aren't able to see them, we can't give them to the people they're intended for. The revelation we receive and the power to bring to pass the words we speak are dependent upon God. The ability to see the revelation He sends, and the ability to correctly interpret and deliver it depends upon us. Prophecy requires both parties to be engaged. God does His part when we do our part.

Not long after I began seeing visions, I was sitting at a restaurant waiting for my order when a woman walked through the door in the company of a man. Out of curiosity (or maybe boredom) I closed my eyes and asked God to show me something about her. I saw a scene with her behaving in a rude and inconsiderate manner toward the man she was with. In this short scene, the Lord revealed some key things about her personality that I would never have known if He had not shown them to me. Now, you might be asking what this information could possibly be used for and that's an excellent question.

If God had shown me the same scene and the woman asked for a prophetic word from me, I would need to consider the type of character He revealed and prophesy to her from what He showed me. I could tell her that the Lord is greatly displeased with the rude way in which she speaks to her husband or boyfriend and admonish her for being disrespectful to Him. But since the purpose of prophecy is to bring encouragement and comfort, I must prophesy to her the opposite spirit of the one I was shown, so to speak. If my discernment was rudeness, I would declare that God's heart was to make her a woman of politeness and gentleness.

Here's another way in which this type of information might be used: If this vision were given to a single man who was looking for a woman to date, he could use the information to decide if she would be someone he might consider dating. A person who inquires of the Lord about the character of those they're interested in dating could benefit from the insights they receive—both positive and negative.

The danger in receiving inside information from God about others is that the information may be used against them for personal reasons. God may disclose the dark secrets of a person's life to any of us. He is no respecter of persons. What the Lord reveals about a person's character is always true; the facts cannot be denied. A person with a desire to tarnish another's reputation can easily use prophetic revelation to "correct" them simply to cause them shame and humiliation. Some believers have been brought before church elders for discipline based on things discerned about them by someone with a score to settle. Before we consider dragging someone's dirty laundry out in the open for public scrutiny, we might ask ourselves how we would feel if we were the one in the hot seat. Prophetic revelation, if it is not used wisely, can cause church splits and destroy life-long friendships. It has as much potential to do harm as good, which is one reason why prophets have been removed from so many churches and the prophetic gifts of the Holy Spirit rejected.

It may be that God will reveal to you issues of sin that people struggle with, but you don't actually need special revelation from God to see people's shortcomings. Most people aren't very good at hiding their faults. It's not hard to confront someone about their religious hypocrisy, their tendency to gossip, or any other weakness, but confrontation seldom produces the results we're after. It typically results in the person feeling like they're being condemned. And since there is no condemnation in Christ (Rom 8:1), any activity that leads to condemnation is counter to the character of Christ's ministry and it should be avoided. The purpose of prophecy is to encourage and exhort the body of Christ. The goal of prophecy then is not to leave a person feeling condemned, but to leave them feeling encouraged. If God reveals a person's sin, we must find a way to handle that revelation in a way that allows us to give them a word that will encourage them.

So how do we accomplish this?

When God shows us a person's sin, He is revealing something about their character. What He reveals in this case is not how He intends for them to live; it is how they happen to be living at the moment. The goal of prophecy is not to expose sin but to inspire righteousness, not to uncover nakedness, but to further clothe with the righteous from the Father. Because the power of the prophetic word is its ability to reveal the future, we must reveal to them the person they will become, and not the person they are today.

If for example, God shows you a vision of a man and his wife, and as the vision progresses a woman appears who seduces the man into having an adulterous affair, we must consider the damage that could be done by accusing him of having an affair, even if the accusation turns out to be true. Prophesying the obvious plans of Satan to destroy his marriage isn't going help him out of the situation he's in. We must prophesy what he doesn't know about God's plans. Instead of building the prophetic word on the plans of the enemy and what success the enemy may have had, we must build the word on the plans of God and the identity and character He has for the man.

God does not orchestrate our failures. He is the author of our faith and the one who brings our sanctification to completion. Each of us has in our spiritual DNA the blueprint for success, but most of us have never seen the blueprint. When we fail, it is because we have allowed the enemy to lead us from the path God has prepared for us (see Jas 1:13). The prophetic word is intended to shine a light upon that path. Knowing that God has prepared a path and a destiny of righteousness for everyone, we must prophesy from the person's divinely ordained destiny, and not their failures. If God shows you a man who is having an affair, you must prophesy that God designed him to be a faithful and loving husband who loves his wife as Christ loves the church (without calling him an adulterer). If God shows you a woman struggling with gossip, you must prophesy from her divine blueprint that God created her to be a loyal and true friend who only speaks encouragement and comfort to her friends. When He shows you images portraying addiction, you have a choice: Do you reveal their addiction and warn them that it displeases God (as if they didn't already know) or do you declare that God's desire is for them to be a pillar of society and a role model for others? The first option will leave them feeling condemned and hopeless, while the second will leave them feeling encouraged.

The prophetic word always calls us to live in a place that is higher than where we are currently living. But it doesn't just call us higher. It carries the power and the anointing of God to make the things we declare come to pass, *if* the hearer chooses to obey them. We must remember that there is real power in the prophetic words we speak. I had an amazing experience with the power of the prophetic word a few years ago. I was in Australia at a meeting with Bruce Lindley, when he approached me and gave me a word from God. I'm not the kind of person who falls down under the power of the Spirit, but as Bruce spoke I felt waves of power hitting me with tremendous force. The force was so strong, it knocked me backward. If it had not been for my wife holding me up, I would have fallen over backward into a row of chairs. Since a prophetic word carries the power to bring to pass what we declare, if we declare a person to be a sinner, we're using the power of the Spirit to reinforce that identity. We must instead use the power of the prophetic word to establish their divine identity and destiny.

I had the opportunity to put this to the test one day. I knew a man who had been a life-long alcoholic, and not just an average one. His alcoholic antics were legendary. His care cost the taxpayers of Washington State tens of millions of dollars over his lifetime. One day I transported him after he had been hospitalized for more than a week. I caught him on a rare day when he was sober. I prophesied the kind of positive things I mentioned above for about ten minutes. I declared that God had not made him an alcoholic, but a man of sobriety. I declared that he would one day be a pillar of society. I told him that he would speak to alcoholics about his own transformation and that his testimony would change their lives. I declared what was not, as if it already was. Shortly after this, he entered alcohol treatment for the 23rd and final time. He's been sober ever since and his testimony of sobriety has inspired many people.

Even though a prophetic word carries the power necessary to make it come to pass, one mistake that many people make is feeling as though God will sovereignly make a prophetic word come to pass with no action being taken on their part. I can't tell you how many of my friends have become disappointed and disgruntled with God because they believed prophetic words that were spoken about their gifting, calling, and relationships which never seemed to materialize as they sat on their couches watching TV. If someone prophesies to you that you're going to have an incredible healing ministry, that prophetic word will never come to pass if you refuse to go out and lay hands on the sick. If someone prophesies that God is bringing you a wise and handsome man of God as your husband, but you do nothing to actually find that man, it is likely that the prophetic word will never come to pass. Prophecy is meant to reveal God's heart for us, but we must always do our part if a prophetic word is going to be fulfilled.

Judging Prophecy

It is our responsibility to judge (or discern) the accuracy of prophetic words. The Bible says:

Let two or three prophets speak, and let the others judge.
1 COR. 14:29

As much as prophecy can encourage us, if it is not handled with discernment, it can cause heartache and frustration. One of the problems with prophecy is that some people get a little too excited about receiving prophetic words and they're afraid to discard any of them—even ones that are obviously inaccurate. We don't do ourselves any favors when we refuse to judge the prophetic words we receive. There's nothing wrong with discarding a word that doesn't bear the witness of the Holy Spirit. We should not feel bad when we dismiss a word someone has spoken to us.

The other problem with prophecy is the fear we tend to have over what others will think of us based on the accuracy of our prophetic words. Even experienced prophets struggle with criticism of the words they've given. There is a tendency for many of us to invest far too much personally, in our own prophetic words. Some of this is done out of a need for self-preservation. It's easy to think that if you give a few words that don't come to pass, you're a lousy prophet or worse— a lousy person. This can create a need to defend our prophetic words to the hilt because our prophetic accuracy determines our value as a person. We should never equate the performance of our ministry with the value of our personhood.

If I allowed myself to be judged by the people I've prayed with who weren't healed or the prophetic words I've given that missed the mark, I'd be considered a miserable failure. But I don't allow myself to be evaluated by my performance in ministry. My value to society isn't determined by whether someone is healed. My value in God's eyes doesn't depend on whether my prophetic words come to pass. All of us will pray for someone who will die without being healed. Everyone who gives prophetic words will have some that miss the mark. None of this means we're any less loved or valued by God. As we mature spiritually, the numbers will mean much less to us and the accuracy of our words will not be an issue that we need to defend as often. We must give people the right to reject the prophetic words we speak, without holding a grudge or being offended. It's only because of insecurity and pride that we might be offended when one of our words is not received.

I personally don't care if someone rejects a prophetic word I've given them. My job is to deliver a message. It's not my concern what they do with it after I give it to them. Frankly, I hope that if it's not an accurate word they toss it in the rubbish bin. Part of the process of maturing in the gift of prophecy is learning to graciously let people off the hook when they don't receive one of our words. I've learned to invest less of myself personally in the prophetic words I give and it's lightened my burden tremendously.

Giving a Prophetic Word

A beautiful illustration of how the prophetic word is intended to work is found in the story of Gideon, taken from the sixth chapter of the book of Judges. The Israelites had been so badly victimized by their enemies, that even the simplest tasks brought fear that they would be further brutalized. Gideon had become so fearful and discouraged that he took to preparing his food in hiding. One day an angel of God came to deliver a word of encouragement to him. The angel called Gideon a mighty man of valor and said that the Lord was with him. Even though at the time, this was not how Gideon saw himself, God saw the man he would become, and sent the angel to declare Gideon's true identity and destiny. God saw Gideon's fears, his insecurity, and his lack of faith, but none of this disappointed or surprised Him. He knew that if Gideon would receive the new identity, all his shortcomings would be removed. The Lord gave a dream to one of the Midianites that was interpreted as a sign of their defeat at the hands of Gideon's army. Gideon, encouraged by the dream, defeated the Midianites in battle. As Gideon obeyed the prophetic word of the angel, he began to take on the divine blueprint that God had prepared for him. This is the power a prophetic word has when it is declared in accordance with God's plans for the person and it is obeyed by them. There are various ways in which we can receive prophetic revelation from God for others, but the one I rely on most looks something like this:

1. I request information from God for an individual.

2. I see the images that He shows me.

3. I either interpret the images and organize them into a set of statements, or alternately, I may not interpret them.

4. I speak them to the person they are for.

Whether or not you interpret the visions God gives you is a decision you must make. Some people will interpret all or most of what they see before they deliver it, while some people will not interpret any of it. Sometimes God will only give you a single word and nothing more. Many times this word will only have a meaning to the person you are prophesying to.

Stacey Campbell told a story about someone who asked her for a word from God. When she closed her eyes, the only thing she received from the Holy Spirit was the word "turkey." She did not feel right about giving a single word, especially such an odd one, so she asked God for more revelation but again she only saw the word "turkey." Somewhat embarrassed, she explained that the only word she received was the word "turkey." She confessed that she did not understand what it meant. The person received it as confirmation about their calling to be a missionary to Turkey.

Once you develop your ability to see in the spirit, this process is not hard to learn. In fact, it may be a good way to learn how to see more clearly, since it provides opportunities to exercise your spiritual senses, which are sharpened when they're used. Most of the prophetic words I've given have come from a set of images God has shown me for a certain person. Typically, I receive three images and from them, I build a prophetic word.

One day I was responding to an email from a friend when I sensed that she needed some encouragement because the enemy had beaten her down. In my mind, I silently asked God for something I could share with her. I closed my eyes and saw three images. The first image was a dreary scene, lit dimly by the cold light that came through a sky covered with thick clouds. The main object in view was a fortress behind a vast perimeter wall. I noticed faint suggestions of dark creatures moving about within the fortress. The second image was of a ball of fire situated in a catapult. In the third scene, the ball of fire was launched into the fortress. When it hit its target the fireball exploded, shooting flames in every direction, which caused the dark creatures to scurry around in a panicked state of confusion. The fire spread and consumed most of the scene before the vision faded to black. How did I give my friend a prophetic word from these scenes?

Step one was to determine whether the images were meant to be taken literally or symbolically. I knew the scenes were not a literal representation of the message, but a symbolic one. Next, I interpreted each scene's meaning. I interpreted the fortress as symbolizing the kingdom of darkness. I interpreted the fireball as a representation of my friend. I felt that she was—metaphorically speaking—a "fireball in the hand of God." This made the interpretation of the last scene fairly easy. God was going to (or already had) launched her into the enemy's camp so that she would cause destruction to the kingdom of darkness. This word hit the mark and years later she recalled the impact it had when she was going through a time of great hardship and discouragement.

Prophetic revelation always has three parts to it. There is the revelation itself, which is the content of the message. The second part is interpretation; we must assign meaning to the revelation so that it can be understood. (The other option is that the one receiving the revelation can interpret it themselves.) The third part is application; this is how the revelation is used by the one it's given to. It is in the application where the power of God comes to bear on the situation spoken of. The will of God for any situation can be frustrated when the revelation He gives is not seen properly, when it is misinterpreted, or when it is misapplied.

One day I received a request for a prophetic word from a friend on one of my social networks. I developed a personal policy about giving prophetic words on social networks because I saw a lot of abuse of the gift of prophecy. Many people have come to treat their prophetic friends like their own personal psychics. Any time they aren't sure what to do about a situation they ask their prophetic friends for a word from God, hoping to receive direction about their situation. They do this I suppose, because they haven't developed confidence in their own ability to hear from God. I want to encourage people to learn to hear God for themselves, so I don't usually give prophetic words on demand, but I felt led to inquire of the Lord for this man to see if He had something to say. I closed my eyes and saw one scene that played like a video in my mind. It was a chaotic scene of people in an indoor children's amusement arcade. There were slides, a bouncy house, and a large ball pit. Each of them had a number of people playing on them. The bouncy house was a particularly hectic-looking scene, with four or five people frantically bouncing around inside of it.

The first step was to determine if the scene was to be taken literally or symbolically. I didn't take it as a literal message, (although it could have been one) but based on what I've learned about the ways of God, I believed it was symbolic. Next, I had to interpret the symbols. We prophesy by faith, so I went with what I believed the Lord was saying in this scene. I typed out what I saw in a private message to my friend and summarized it in one word—chaos. I then went on to explain it in more detail. I believed the Lord was saying that my friend's mind was being bombarded by many chaotic thoughts and that he was having a hard time shutting down his mind and having peace. I suggested that the chaos is not how God wants him to live—that it's a problem that needs to be remedied—and that he needs to find a way to enter deeper into God's rest. He replied that what I had seen in the vision and how I interpreted it was exactly how he had been feeling. My words served as confirmation on an issue God had already been speaking to him about.

The Office of Prophet

There is a distinction that must be made between the gift of prophecy which is utterance given by inspiration of the Holy Spirit to believers, and the gift of the prophet, that is given by Jesus. It seems as though the gifts of Jesus, which are mentioned in Ephesians chapter four are actually people and their particular ministries. These individuals are commonly referred to as those who occupy the "office" of the prophet, evangelist, teacher, pastor, and apostle. The New Testament prophet has a role that is quite different from his Old Testament counterpart, because he operates under a new and better covenant (see Heb 8:6).

The nature of prophecy as described in first Corinthians applies to the office of the prophet. Though the purpose for prophecy remains the same—to bring edification and encouragement—the prophet generally operates in a wider scope than the believer who prophesies. The effectiveness of a prophet can be hindered by the belief that their primary function is to prophesy. The model of the prophet who travels near and far delivering prophetic warnings to disobedient people, which is so commonly found in the Old Testament, is not the main function of prophets today. The primary function of the New Testament prophet (some would argue this was the intended function of the Old Testament prophet) is training and equipping the saints for the work of ministry. And while part of that training and equipping may involve dispensing prophetic words when prompted, the greater part of the workload of the prophet is helping the body of Christ to grow in spiritual maturity.

I was talking with a young friend one day who was excited about what he felt was his calling as a prophet. As we discussed our views on the purpose of prophets and prophecy, he said he felt like it was his responsibility to uncover the secret sins of pastors and other church leaders that God would send him to. He believed God's purpose for his ministry was to confront leaders to let them know that God was aware of what they were doing in secret and that He wasn't going to put up with it anymore. This young man had been influenced by a more seasoned prophet who felt he had the same calling. These men traveled in a circle of friends, all of whom felt the same way about the ministry of the prophet. Their sub-culture endorsed a model of prophetic ministry where itinerant prophets go from church to church delivering messages of not-so-happy news and confronting people about their secret sins. These prophets usually have no ties to the churches where they prophesy and seldom (if ever) develop meaningful relationships with the people they prophesy to.

I'd like to make it absolutely clear that I'm not in favor of people having their lives destroyed by sin. But I'm not sure it's the responsibility of prophets to sniff out the sins of others and confront them publicly. While this approach may have been used at times by prophets of the old covenant, it often produced poor fruit, seldom achieving the effects the prophets intended. Prophets are intended to be leaders. Leadership is a matter being granted influence in someone's life. Relationships built on trust give you influence in the lives of others. Prophets are more likely to have opportunities to train and equip their communities when they develop relationships built on trust and that's difficult to do if you feel it's your job to confront people about their sin. It's the Holy Spirit's job to convict and correct people of sin. Our job is to love and encourage them.

Living in the community where you prophesy, compells you to take a measure of responsibility for seeing the effects of your prophetic words come to pass. A prophet who prophesies to a community hundreds of miles from home has no personal stake in the future of that town, no reason to intercede for them, and no obligation to help people walk the path God has set before them. Even the prophets of the old covenant lived in the communities and had relationships with the people they prophesied to. The story of the rebuilding of the temple following Israel's captivity illustrates of how the prophets of God took a personal interest in seeing their community's vision come to pass.

After a long journey back to the Promised Land, the Israelites encountered a small group of people bent on keeping them from rebuilding the temple. Led by their governor Tattenai, the locals continually criticized the Israelites in an effort to inhibit the work of the Lord. They went so far as to hire people to taunt the Israelites and urged King Darius to tell them to cease their work. Speaking to the discouraged Israelites, Haggai and Zechariah prophesied to them that despite Tattenai's discouragement, the time had come to rebuild. After hearing the word of the prophets, the work of rebuilding began:

> *So Zerubbabel rose up and began to build the house of God which is in Jerusalem; and the prophets of God were with them, helping them.*
> EZ 5:2

The prophets, whose main job was to hear from God, picked up their shovels and hammers and went to work beside their brothers.

I'd like to share a story about a prophetic word I gave that surprised me. It also surprised the people who received it. After spending nine days in the Pacific Northwest with friends, my wife and I got on the plane back to Phoenix and stowed our bags in the overhead bin. Most of the passengers had already boarded the plane. I sat down and soon heard the unmistakable cry of a baby coming from the seat behind me. I looked at my wife. "Well, that's cool. We get to sit in front of a screaming baby."

I had not slept well the night before. The hotel room became too warm, so at one o'clock in the morning I got up and opened the window then went to the lobby for a drink of water. I fell back into a fitful sleep until the alarm went off. By the time we got to the airport, I was tired and a bit grouchy. I did my best to rest on the plane, but the coughing and crying of the child in the seat behind us made it hard to rest and I found myself becoming more annoyed as time went on.

An hour before the plane landed, I began feeling a vibration in my right leg near where I keep my cell phone. Every two minutes or so it felt like my phone was alerting me. I checked my phone several times for new messages, but there were none. There couldn't be. At 30,000 feet my phone couldn't receive a signal from a cell tower. I began thinking that maybe the vibration was coming from the Lord and He was trying to get my attention. So I closed my eyes and saw some images and a few words in my mind, but I didn't see any clear messages that I could understand. I tried again to rest, but the vibration in my leg continued every few minutes.

After the flight attendants had put away the beverage carts, the baby began a tirade of non-stop screaming that was unsettling his parents and getting on the nerves of people around us. When a baby flies in an airplane it doesn't know that swallowing will equalize the pressure in the ears. He's going to feel pain in his ears from atmospheric pressure changes. Who could blame him for crying? In spite of this, his parents seemed terribly ashamed that he was creating an inconvenience for the rest of the passengers.

I closed my eyes again and this time I saw a clear message from God in my mind. In white letters on a black background I saw the words, "Pray for my peace to overcome the child." I thought to myself, I can do that. As I prayed, I kept my eyes closed and to my surprise, I saw an image in my mind of Jesus approaching the child and cuddling him. I continued praying, and as I watched this happen in my mind, the baby's screaming coming from behind me slowly subsided. Then, in a clear thought impression that seemed foreign to me, I heard the Lord say one more thing. "Tell his parents that I have heard their cries and I will give them everything they have asked for."

Now if God told you to tell a perfect stranger something like this you might hesitate to share it with them. Some of us would try to rationalize it away and tell ourselves, that was definitely not God or reason that He would never say something like that. I had a little apprehension about sharing what I saw and heard. As the plane descended into Phoenix I began to feel an unusual compassion for the baby's parents that made my eyes fill with tears. I knew it was the Lord showing me how He felt about them.

As the plane taxied to the terminal, I asked the child's parents if I might give them an encouraging word about their future. They said they would be glad to hear one. I said, "About an hour ago when your son was crying, God asked me to pray for the peace of Jesus to overcome him. I began praying for that and as I did, the Lord asked me to tell you, 'Just as all the people on this plane have heard the cries of your child, I have heard your cries and I will give you all you have asked for.' The Lord's heart toward you is full of compassion. He has not forgotten you. He will never forsake you. He will bring to pass all that He promised you. So I hope you've dreamed big, because He's going to make your dreams come true." They thanked me, and as I exited the plane I gave the boy's father a hug.

Keep your eyes and ears open for opportunities to bless strangers with a word from God. I was not in a mood to bless anyone when this encounter began, and it took a lot of prompting from God to get my attention. Once you develop a relationship with Him, you can talk with Him about any subject you'd talk to a friend about, including the people around you. You might be surprised at what He'll show you.

Exercise

The next time you're with a friend or relative, ask if they might be willing to receive a prophetic word from you. If they agree, ask the Holy Spirit to show you something about them and deliver a word of encouragement to them based on what He shows you. Ask if they sense that the revelation was truly from the heart of God.

Notes

CHAPTER TEN

Seeing in the Spirit and Healing

ONE OF THE MOST COMMON reasons why the Holy Spirit will show us things in the spirit is to assist us in the ministry of healing. I'd like to provide a brief summary of the dynamics of divine healing:

When the Roman Centurion asked Jesus to heal his servant, he knew Jesus had authority to heal, and he knew Jesus only needed to say a word and his servant would be healed. Here is one of the keys to healing—it's an issue of authority. Jesus marveled that the servant had such a keen understanding of authority and that he had such great faith. No prayer was involved in the healing; Jesus spoke a word and the servant was healed. It was a simple transaction involving the faith of the Centurion and the authority of Jesus (see Mt 8:5-13).

Although they used slightly different approaches with each healing encounter, Jesus and the disciples usually spoke a word of healing, touched a sick person, or in some way transferred power to them. They never asked the Father to heal the sick. They understood that healing power of God resided *in* them and it flowed *to* those who needed healing. A few passages from the New Testament make a simple outline for understanding how we are to operate in healing:

Jesus chose twelve disciples and commissioned them to go out to the cities of Israel. These were His instructions to them:

> *And as you go, preach, saying, 'The kingdom of heaven is at hand.'*
> *Heal the sick, cleanse the lepers, raise the dead, cast out demons.*
> MT. 10:7-8

He gave them authority over all the power of the enemy:

> *Behold, I give you the authority to trample on serpents and*
> *scorpions, and over all the power of the enemy, and nothing shall*
> *by any means hurt you.*
> LK. 10:19

After He was resurrected He told them they would receive power:

> *But you shall receive power when the Holy Spirit has come upon*
> *you; and you shall be witnesses to Me in Jerusalem, and in all*
> *Judea and Samaria, and to the end of the earth.*
> ACTS 1:8

Jesus gave His disciples assignments for healing, deliverance, and raising the dead, and He gave them the power and authority they would need to carry out the assignments. Let's have a closer look at the power and authority He gave them.

Authority to Heal

The Greek word for "authority" which is found in the passage I quoted above (Lk. 10:19) is the Greek word, *exousia*. This is the most commonly used New Testament word for authority. Strong's concordance gives the following definitions for this word:

1. power of choice, liberty of doing as one pleases
   a. leave or permission

2. physical and mental power
   a. the ability or strength with which one is endued, which he either possesses or exercises

Power to Heal

Jesus said His disciples would receive power when the Holy Spirit came upon them. What kind of power did they receive? The word translated "power" in the passage I quoted above (Acts 1:8) is the Greek word *dunamis*. Strong's concordance gives the following definitions:

1. strength, power, ability
   a. inherent power, power residing in a thing by virtue of its nature, or which a person or thing exerts and puts forth
   b. power for performing miracles
   c. power consisting in or resting upon armies, forces, hosts

These definitions speak of power and authority that reside within the individual. The authority we have is the legal right to do the things Jesus told us to do. The power He gave to us is the operation of the Holy Spirit within us. Once we've been given the power and authority to heal the sick, we never need to ask God to do it for us. We have the power and authority to do it ourselves. While the power and authority to heal are ultimately tied to the authority of Christ, they are given to and may be exercised freely by us. This power and authority is how Jesus and the disciples healed people in the first century and it is no different for us today.

If you're praying with someone who needs healing, you might be shown a scene where they're suffering abuse or neglect. You might see them in a car accident that caused a neck or back injury. When God shows you an image of someone as they may have looked when they were in a car accident, the information is given so that you'll have some background information to work with. When you ask a stranger if they were in a car accident they're usually surprised that you knew this without them telling you. If the image you're shown highlights a certain part of the body that was injured, like the neck, and you ask if they have neck pain, the information provides hope that God intends to heal them.

The visions God will show you may look like an x-ray image where you see broken bones highlighted, detached tendons, or even tumors. In cases like these, God is showing you a key to the person's healing. When I see images portraying injury or sickness, I know it's time for me to focus on getting the person healed. When you see tumors, command them to leave. When you see broken bones, command them to be healed, when you see emotional trauma or abuse, you may need to spend time doing emotional healing. (In most cases you can use the exercise at the end of chapter five.)

I usually pray for the person from whatever I see happening in the vision. As I pray, the vision usually changes according to the effects of my prayer. If I see a tumor, I'll begin to pray (most of the time I'm commanding it to leave) and it usually begins to shrink as I continue watching it in the vision. I continue praying until I can no longer see it. If I see a deformed wrist, I pray until the person feels no more pain or the image of their wrist in the vision looks normal. Sometimes the person will feel no change in their level of pain as I'm praying. If I see information in the vision that indicates the healing is done, I'll stop praying and believe they are healed. By following up with people I've prayed with weeks later, I've learned that even if they felt nothing when I prayed, in most cases their symptoms eventually left.

Sometimes in a vision, God will show me someone having difficulty breathing. When He does, I'll pray for healing of their heart and lungs until I see them breathing normally in the vision. I've seen people with severe emphysema healed this way. Sometimes I'll see a glowing ball of light enter a person's body that travels around inside of them as I pray for their healing. (The ball of light that I'm shown is a symbolic representation of God's healing power, provided for my benefit.) When I prayed for my brother who had cancer that had spread to several organs of his body, I prayed for hours in the hospital. During this time, I saw a golden ball of light passing through his bladder, his liver and the other organs that were affected by cancer. When I see something like this, I continue praying until I see the ball of light leave them.

Praying for healing in this manner does not require you to be in the same room with the one you're praying for. I receive many prayer requests by e-mail from people around the world. When I receive a prayer request, I close my eyes and look to see what God wants to show me. Sometimes I see the person I'm praying for standing or sitting in front of me in a vision and I'll see a glowing ball of light begin to travel around inside their body. One day I prayed this way for a man in Africa who had malaria. He reported the next day that all his symptoms disappeared overnight. I use this method of prayer nearly every day.

I had an opportunity to pray in person with a friend who had suffered from Lyme disease for many years. As I prayed with her, I saw in my mind's eye something that looked like a round circle of light like you would see if you were looking through a microscope. Inside the circle of light, I saw small black specks that resembled bacteria. There appeared to be at least 100 of them. I assumed that what I saw was a representation of the organism that caused the disease. (There really is no way around making these kinds of assumptions. If you want to see people healed you have to make some assumptions and take a few risks.) I commanded the black specks to die and as I did, they slowly disappeared from my view. After about ten minutes of commanding them to die, I could no longer see any of them. All I saw was an empty circle of light. I told my friend that I was done praying and that I thought she was healed. Six months later I checked up on her condition and to her surprise, she had completely forgotten that she even had Lyme disease because she had experienced no outbreaks since the night I prayed with her.

I'd like to share a testimony of my own healing that involved information the Lord showed me in several visions. For many years, my body showed signs of a medical condition that I recognized as paroxysmal supraventricular tachycardia (PSVT.) In this condition, the heart has an extra pathway that allows electrical impulses to flow through it at a very fast rate. During episodes of PSVT, the heart rate can rise to over 200 beats per minute. Another characteristic is that it comes on for no apparent reason. I knew the condition was treatable with medication to control the heart rate or by having an "ablation" procedure performed, which destroys the pathway that causes the increased heart rate. I never wanted to be officially diagnosed and never spoke to my own doctor about it, but I had discussed treatment options with a cardiologist I met at work.

I was very reluctant to even consider receiving treatment for this condition. I was content to manage it myself. When I was younger, I could make an episode of PSVT go away by coughing or holding my breath, but as I grew older these measures were of no help. For many years, I remained in limbo about this health issue, not wanting to see a doctor because I had seen the side effects some patients suffer with medication or ablation. Later in my life, when I became convinced that God wanted to heal us of our medical problems I began asking Him to heal my heart.

I attended a spiritual conference in Spokane, Washington on the last weekend of September in 2009. My wife and I went there hoping to be healed of chronic neck and back pain. I went forward to the stage area during worship; it was a powerful experience. When I closed my eyes I saw a vision of a credit card and silver and gold coins. Based on my history of visions from God, I believed He was asking me to give a large donation that night. I asked about a specific amount to give, but He didn't give me a number. After worship, I made my way back to my seat. I began to discuss the donation amount with my wife and she got out our checkbook.

"How much should we donate?"

"How much did we give last night?" I asked. She leaned over and whispered the amount in my ear.

"Well maybe we should give ten times that much."

My wife is usually the one who is prompted by God with an amount to give. We discussed it and she began writing the date and payee on the check. Before she filled in the amount, I went into an episode of PSVT. My heart quickly hit a racing speed and I broke out in a sweat. I tried coughing and holding my breath but it wasn't helping, so I told my wife what was happening. She took one look at me, promptly dropped the checkbook, and began to lay hands on me in prayer. Friends and people sitting near us quickly joined in.

The pounding in my chest felt like someone was hitting me with a hammer, making it hard to breathe. A volunteer noticed what was going on and asked if I wanted them to call for an ambulance. I sensed God wanted to do something and the last thing I needed was a visit to the emergency department. I said, "No, don't call. I'm a paramedic." About 20 minutes went by and nothing had changed. God spoke to me again about making a large donation through another vision of credit cards and coins. I sensed my healing was hovering over me and it would come when I took a step of faith. I turned to my wife and said, "Stop praying for me and fill out the check."

She seemed stunned that I would want her to stop praying and really didn't like the idea of putting the donation ahead of my healing. Turning to the woman sitting next to her, she asked her to pray for me in her place. Because I seemed so serious about it, she grabbed the checkbook off the floor and filled in our offering amount. I was watching her write the numbers and as soon as she filled in the dollar amount, the episode of PSVT ended. We all breathed a sigh of relief and gave a shout of praise to God. As I sat there, I began to realize that I was permanently healed of my condition.

The Word of Knowledge

The "word of knowledge" is one of the gifts of the holy Spirit mentioned in first Corinthians:

For to one is given the word of wisdom through the Spirit, to another the word of knowledge through the same Spirit,
1 COR 12:8

A word of knowledge is revelation from the Holy Spirit about certain facts that we have no knowledge of. Actually, the same is true for the word of wisdom. The difference is that the word of knowledge tells us the facts about a situation, while a word of wisdom tells us what do about it. A word of knowledge can come in a number of different ways. Some people hear the voice of God speaking through thought impressions in their mind. Others receive them through dreams or visions. Some people receive them through their other senses. A word of knowledge for healing sometimes presents as a sudden pain in our body without an injury or illness to cause it. The area of the body that hurts corresponds to an injury or illness in the same part of the body that someone else has. Our pain is God's way of telling us that He desires to heal them. Once we pray for them to be healed, the sensation of pain will leave. If the word of knowledge comes as a visual image, it may remain in our mind until we act upon it. Learning to receive words of knowledge will come as we develop greater sensitivity to the leading of the Holy Spirit and as we develop our ability to see in the spirit by exercise.

Words of knowledge can come in the form of literal words that you see in your mind. They might be anything from a person's name, to the kind of sickness they have, to their favorite flavor of ice cream. Words of knowledge are frequently about an illness or injury that God wants to heal. One of the first words of knowledge I ever received came while I was standing in line at a grocery store. I felt the presence of God move me slightly and took it as a cue that there was someone He wanted me to pray with. I closed my eyes and immediately saw the word "Headaches" in white letters on a black background in my mind. The word remained there for a few seconds then it was replaced with a front-view portrait of a middle-aged woman with blonde hair. I took note of her and when I opened my eyes I realized she was the woman standing in line in front of me. I'm not the smartest person in the world, but I put two and two together and assumed she had headaches that God wanted to heal. I asked if she wanted her headaches healed and she did. We prayed and since she was an employee at the store I was able to check up on her periodically. She hasn't had a migraine head-ache since that day.

A word of knowledge can be combined with a word of wisdom to help solve a problem. One of the more unusual words of knowledge I received was about a problem I had while repairing my car. I had been working on my car for several days and had just finished replacing the timing belt. After putting everything back together, the car wouldn't start. I checked the service manual to verify that I had the timing mark on the camshaft in the right position, but I couldn't find the problem. Everything seemed to be where it should be according to the service manual. I didn't know what to do next and became very frustrated. But then I closed my eyes and asked God to show me what was wrong. In a vision in my mind's eye, I saw the camshaft gear and noticed that it had two timing marks on it. I was aware of only one. The mark I had used as a reference point was the wrong one. After locating the other timing mark and making the correction, I started up the car and it ran perfectly. If I had not calmed myself down, closed my eyes and asked God to show me the problem, I probably wouldn't have been able to get the car running without taking it to a mechanic.

Once you're seeing in the spirit you may find God highlighting certain people whom He wants to draw to your attention. You might see them highlighted in a kind of spotlight that makes them stand out from the rest of the crowd. I frequently see pictures of people in my mind when I close my eyes. I had a seasoned prophet instruct me to sit in the last row of seats when I attend a church service to get a better view of the congregation. He found that during a service God will bring certain people to his attention and give him words of knowledge and prophetic insights about them. He writes down the names of the people God highlights and makes notes on the revelation he receives about them so that after the service he can deliver the words to those who are willing to receive them. I've found that especially during worship, God will give me visual images of certain people that He either wants me to pray with or give a prophetic word to.

When I first became interested in healing, I always asked God if He would heal a person before praying with them. I had very little faith for healing at the time and I was afraid of praying for the wrong person. One day I transported a patient who had many different medical conditions. The transport to the hospital would only take a few minutes. I asked God if He would heal her, closed my eyes and to my shock I saw the words, "I will not heal." I wasn't sure I saw correctly, so I closed my eyes and asked again and saw the same words. Since God had commissioned me to pray for my patients and said He would heal them, I asked why He wouldn't heal her. What followed made it perfectly clear. I closed my eyes and saw a frightening scene that included a monster resembling Frankenstein's creature that was at least 100 feet tall, another creature resembling a mummy and several ghoulish creatures running down the street. Finally I saw a massive dragon flying in front of a city skyscraper. All of this was played out on a dark, sickly-looking background.

These images helped me understand that this woman had so many demons that needed to be removed before she could be healed that I simply didn't have the time required to do the work of deliverance and healing in the short time we would be in the ambulance. I'd like to make one point clear: God did not tell me He *could not* heal this woman. He said He *would not* heal her and it was not because He didn't *want* her to be healed, but because her healing—if she were to keep it—would require a much longer process than I had time for. God may not always answer our "why" questions, but there are times when He'll probably give you an explanation. One of those times is when He's instructed you to do something and He makes an exception to the orders He's already given you. At those times, it seems reasonable to ask why, lest you become confused about what He expects of you.

It's not unusual when I pray for a person who needs healing to see flames either inside of them or around them. Although all prophetic symbolism has the potential to carry either a negative or positive meaning, most of the time when I see flames in the context of healing it represents the healing "fire of God" at work in them as I pray. Context is important and it should always be considered when determining the way in which a vision is interpreted and applied.

Very often when I pray for healing of back pain, in a vision, I'll see a column of fire along the person's spine. This information serves two purposes. It lets me know that God is healing that part of their body, which increases my faith that they'll be healed. But it also tells me what the person is probably feeling as I pray, and since I like to talk with people when I pray with them, I'll usually ask if they're feeling heat along their spine. If they say "yes" I explain that it's the power of God healing them. In the same way, I sometimes see either flames or what appear to be waves of heat around an injured part of the body such as a sprained wrist. The same principle applies. I usually take this as a confirmation that the power of God is healing that part of the body and discuss the progression of their healing based on what I see.

When I pray for healing, I often see people with snakes wrapped around them. Sometimes I'll see dozens of snakes coming out of a person's body and other times I might see one large python. Sometimes I'll see a serpent coiled up looking at me. To the untrained person, serpents may not mean much, but I've learned that when God shows me serpents in the context of healing, it usually represents the presence of one or more demons that must be removed before the healing can take place. In these cases, I direct my prayer at evicting the demons and I don't stop until all indications of them are gone. I command them to leave and I don't quit until there are no more snakes visible in the vision that I'm seeing. The same principle applies when God shows me spiders, scorpions, or any other venomous creature. Anything that God shows you that appears to be poisonous—something that could be lethal if it attacked you—should be taken as a warning of the presence of something dangerous. The danger may be anything from witchcraft to the presence of evil spirits, but consider that you may also be dealing with an actual poisoning from a bite or sting. Sometimes visions of venomous creatures should be interpreted literally. Don't be afraid to ask the Holy Spirit if you're not certain how one of these creatures that you see in a vision should be interpreted.

Healing as Seen From the Spiritual Perspective

A friend came to visit me in Arizona for a few days, but he forgot to bring a pair of shorts. I broke my coffeemaker a couple days after he arrived so a trip to the Goodwill store was in order. After a few minutes of browsing through the store he found his shorts, I picked up a slightly used Mr. Coffee and we headed for the checkout. The woman in front of us at the checkout stand happened to be in a wheelchair. I made small talk with her before she left and I thought this would be a good opportunity to teach my friend about healing. Now, it's not like he's never seen anyone healed—he has. He just hasn't had as many opportunities as I have and I promised him a one-on-one healing lesson which I never made good on in the past. So here was an opportunity to give him a demonstration sitting right in front of us.

We followed the woman outside and introduced ourselves. I told her I was teaching my friend about healing. (Great cover story by the way and it's not a lie.) We asked if we might pray with her for healing. She was delighted that we asked. It turns out she was diagnosed with polio more than 60 years ago. We prayed for a few minutes, but she showed no outward signs of being healed. She thanked us and we went on our way. On the way to the car I told him, "We just tossed another log on her fire."

He replied, "Tell me more." (He says that a lot.)

We had a discussion in the car about the process of healing. I explained that contrary to what most of us have been taught, healing is not usually a "one time" thing that happens to us. It's generally an ongoing process. Even the miracles of healing that we occasionally witness are not usually what they appear to be. Let me explain what I mean by that:

A friend once made the observation that "all the healing in the Bible was instant healing." I didn't correct them, but if you want to know the truth about how healing happened when Jesus and the disciples prayed for people, I would suggest reading the healing accounts from scriptures carefully without adding preconceived ideas to the text. You'll probably notice that not all the healing accounts were recorded as being instant miracles. In the vast majority of cases, the Bible simply says Jesus healed a multitude of people. There is no description of how most of them were healed and no indication of whether the healings were gradual or instantaneous. Even in some cases where individual healings were recorded, the writer simply states that the person was healed. No information is given about whether the healing took ten seconds, ten minutes or two hours. The lack of details about how these people were healed leaves the issue open for discussion.

Most of us perceive miracles and healing as something that happens to us once, which never needs to happen again. While it is true that a broken bone for example, might be healed miraculously and the individual may never have a problem with it again, there are other conditions that must be considered. If your condition happens to be asthma, insomnia, or irritable bowel syndrome, you might be healed of the condition once, only to have the symptoms return a few months later.

It is my belief that many of these conditions are caused by evil spirits, while things like broken bones are not. The fever that Peter's mother had which Jesus rebuked seemed to be an example of a sickness caused by a spirit (see Lk 4:39). If the fever were not some sort of spirit, then why was it rebuked? Once we've been set free of a spirit of illness, there is no guarantee that the same or a different spirit won't return later to afflict us. The return of the spirit brings a return of the symptoms, and the return of the symptoms requires another round of prayer, which is why I see healing more as an ongoing process than a single event. Healing is similar to the process of sanctification, which the Holy Spirit does not accomplish in us all at once.

We are made righteous in God's eyes the moment we receive Jesus as our Savior. We can never become more righteous in terms of how God sees us than we are the moment we believe. But the transformational work of God in us, which creates Christ-like character, is a gradual process. While there are often dramatic events during the process of sanctification—like an alcoholic whose desire to drink is removed instantly—the entire work the Holy Spirit does in each of us takes time. His work of healing is much the same way. We might have an occasional instant breakthrough in one area or another, but the greater healing process that God does is always being worked out over time.

Few of us are able to see God's supernatural work of healing as it happens. And because we can't see it, we often assume nothing is happening when we pray for someone who shows no outward signs of healing. But if we were able to see in the spirit, we would be amazed. When we pray even the smallest, most feeble prayer for someone, we release a measure of God's glory upon them. When I pray for a person's healing I often see angels being released to combat evil spirits. I see wounds that have been inflicted by the enemy visibly healed in their soul, and the countenance of their spirit visibly changed, even though nothing appears to be happening outwardly. If we only knew the mighty and wonderful things that were taking place in the spirit when we pray, we would not think so little of our prayers.

I'd like to share a story about a patient I transported that illustrates how God can use dreams and visions to speak to people about what's happening with their health. One day my EMT partner and I responded to a call to the Mayo Hospital in Scottsdale, Arizona. On the way to the call I pulled out my phone and searched online for the diagnosis we got from dispatch as my partner drove. I'd never heard of NDMA encephalopathy. Wikipedia said it's a rare autoimmune disease that typically affects young women, and is often associated with ovarian tumors. The onset is usually gradual, with altered mental status, seizures, and eventually coma. The long term prognosis is good if properly diagnosed and treated.

We arrived at the ICU to find Monica (not her real name) lying in bed. The first thing I noticed was that her facial muscles were in a constant state of twitching. She was unable to respond to me. Her father and mother introduced themselves and explained her condition. Monica's father is a paramedic instructor from a small town in Texas. They brought her to Mayo because it's one of the only hospitals in the Southwest with the ability to treat her condition.

As people wandered in and out of the room, her nurse gave me report. From an envelope, she pulled out a thick stack of papers that were stapled together and handed them to me. "Here," she said, "You need to give these to the people who will be taking care of her where she's going."

"Uh, okay," I said. "Can I ask what these papers are?"

"Sure. This is going to sound a little weird, but for the past four months, all of us nurses who have been taking care of Monica have been recording everything she's gone through. Every shift we've been taking turns writing notes on her progress and we put everything into a journal that has to stay with her."

The stack of papers was not part of her hospital medical record. It was a group journal the nurses decided to do on their own, to keep track of her progress. As I read the notes, I smiled. They recorded all of her procedures, every seizure she had, and every change in mental status. This was all in addition to the charting they did for the hospital. I noticed that Monica's finger nails were painted. The nail polish looked fresh. An attractive pink stripe pattern adorned each nail. "Who did her nails?" I asked.

"We all did!" One of the nurses replied. The room had quickly filled with nurses, techs, and other employees who wanted to see her off. I can't recall ever seeing a group of nurses who became so involved in the personal life of their patient. It was like they had adopted her as a sister. We carefully moved Monica to the gurney and got her covered and belted in for the trip. The loving people from Mayo bade her farewell as we rolled her to the elevator. Her mother was riding with us. Inside the ambulance, I asked if I could pray for her daughter. Her mother replied, "By all means, please do!"

I closed my eyes and placed my hand on her shoulder and declared life over her. In my mind's eye I immediately saw Monica sitting up with her eyes open talking to her mother, as if nothing was wrong. I commanded sickness to leave and for her immune system to be healed. We both prayed for this lively young woman trapped inside a broken body. After I was finished I turned to her mother. "Can I tell you what I saw when I was praying?"

"Of course you can. I'd be very interested in hearing about what you saw."

"As I prayed, God showed me a vision of Monica. She was sitting up on the gurney talking to you like nothing was wrong with her. I think it means that she's aware of what's going on around her." I shared with her some of the visions I had seen during prayer and a few of the dreams I'd had about my patients.

She smiled. "It's funny you mentioned dreams. The nurses at Mayo have been having dreams about Monica ever since she arrived. In the dreams, they're always talking to her as if she's perfectly healthy. They believe the dreams were a reminder to let them know that she can understand everything they were saying, in spite of how things look. The dreams are one reason why all the nurses took such an interest in her and why they've treated her like a sister."

This encounter helped me understand that God is much more willing to communicate through dreams and visions than we realize. I received this message from Monica's mother a few months later:

Hi!

Just wanted to give you a little update. She is now in an out-patient day program, is volunteering at the humane society, and they are actually talking about her starting back at school in the fall! PLEASE feel free to use her story as an example of God's wonderful work as you continue to minister (both physically and spiritually) to others.

Thanks again,

Liz

Let me share one more story: I'm often at the bedside of people who are terminally ill or who have suffered cardiac arrest. One of the things people want to know is whether the person is going to recover or not. Many times I've prayed at a person's bedside and as I closed my eyes, saw a vision of a heavenly scene. Sometimes I saw angels descending to usher the person into heaven. Other times I saw Jesus interacting with them. Most visions like these indicate that the person is heaven-bound. One day a friend asked me to accompany him to a hospital to pray for a friend who was in the ICU. He had suffered cardiac arrest and was successfully resuscitated, but he was in a coma. My friend wanted me to do two things: The first was to pray for his friend to be healed and to have a full recovery, but he also wanted to me to take a peek into the spiritual realm and tell him what I saw.

As I stood beside the bed in the ICU with about a half-dozen friends and family members present, I prayed for his healing. I closed my eyes and sure enough, in a vision that I saw in my mind, I saw him sitting up in bed talking to the people in the room as if nothing was wrong with him. I looked at my friend and asked, "Would you like to know what I'm seeing?"

"I think we would all like to know," he replied.

"Well, I see him sitting up in bed talking with everyone as if there's nothing wrong with him. He looks pretty happy and as far as I can tell—pretty normal. I'll go out on a limb and say that I think he's going to recover from this." The group was encouraged by what I told them. In all the years I've been doing this with very sick people—whether it looks like they'll be stepping into eternity or recovering from their illness—a prophetic look at the outcome is always welcome. It usually confirms what friends and family have been thinking and sometimes it helps in the process of transition or making plans for the future.

Appearances Can be Deceiving

Things that you see in the spirit can take on different appearances from one moment to the next. You might see a tall and ferocious-looking demon confronting you one minute, but after you rebuke the spirit, it may gradually look more like a small and harmless cloud of dirt. Spiritual beings are able to change their appearance to varying degrees. Angels can take on many different appearances. They can appear as a translucent being of light one minute, and a moment later take on the appearance of an ordinary man or woman.

I have several friends who have made some breakthroughs in the area of deliverance and inner healing by utilizing the power of prophetic acts that are based on what they see in the spirit. One friend, Matt Evans, has trained himself to see in the spirit with very good accuracy. Seeing is one thing, but knowing what to do with what you see is another. Matt frequently sees devices attached to people that represent demonic tools and implements of oppression. He told me about a woman he saw on the street that was walking in front of him. In the spirit, he saw a metal band fastened around her head. He decided to perform a prophetic act to cut the metal band off. Imagining in his spirit that he was holding a tool that could cut the band, by faith, he made the motion of cutting the band with the tool. Immediately after doing this, the woman exclaimed that she suddenly felt her headache disappear. God had revealed to Matt a spiritual problem that required a prophetic act to bring relief.

People with well-developed spiritual vision sometimes see swords and spears impaled in others. They may see people tied up in chains and all sorts of other devices of torment and torture. A prophetic act to remove the devices along with prayer for the affected person will often bring healing. Most people who are accustomed to living by the laws of the physical world do not understand how an "imaginary" tool can be used to remove an "imaginary" band around someone's head to relieve a headache. Equally puzzling is when a short healing prayer combined with a prophetic act to remove an "imaginary" spear brings relief of someone's pain. Just because something is not visible in the physical world does not mean it is not real. The words "invisible" and "imaginary" do not mean the same thing. Angels and demons are not usually visible in the physical world, but they are just as real as you or me. Paul wrote to believers in Corinth:

"We do not look at the things which are seen, but at the things which are not seen. For the things which are seen are temporary, but the things which are not seen are eternal."
2 COR 4:18

Tools, devices, castles, mountains, rivers, dragons, demons, torture chambers, or anything else you might see in the spirit have a real entity associated with them. While the image you see may not perfectly represent the object or being you're dealing with, the being or object it represents will respond to whatever you do to or with it in the spirit.

As I mentioned in an earlier chapter, thoughts in the spirit world are creative in nature. They are composed of the spiritual light of eternity that originates in the glory of God. When we speak of creative thought, we're not speaking of the "creative visualization" used by Buddhists and New Age practitioners, nor are we referring to the "positive thinking" that has been promoted by self-help gurus to imagine the circumstances they desire. We're talking about the kingdom of heaven empowering the human spirit to manifest the realities of heaven in both the physical and spiritual realms.

A prophetic act done in faith can create a reality in the spiritual world that has an effect in the physical world. Faith carries a lot more weight than we realize. It's the currency of heaven that purchases—and in some cases creates—the realities we experience in the physical world. If you need a reminder of the power of faith, take a walk through the eleventh chapter of the book of Hebrews.

Steve Harmon found a brilliant way to put this reality into practice. One day he was ministering healing to a person with Dissociative Identity Disorder. He had been working with them for a long time and he was essentially teaching one of the soul's children (sometimes called alters) about God. During these encounters, Steve asks Jesus to assist in the process. The session was nearing an end and the person wanted to know what they should do until their next session. Steve asked Jesus for advice. Jesus told him to create a book about God for them to read.

Steve asked Jesus, "How do I do that?" Jesus told him to speak it into existence. Using his imagination, Steve spoke into existence a spiritual book then handed it to the alter and told him to read it. When they met during the next session, the alter told Steve the things he had learned about God by reading the book.

I'd briefly like to discuss how our understanding of the spiritual world impacts the ministry of emotional healing. People who have Dissociative Identity Disorder (formerly known as Multiple Personality Disorder) have souls that have been fragmented due to emotional trauma. The nature of fragmentation is more complicated than I can explain here, but suffice it to say that there are greater and lesser degrees of fragmentation. Smaller parts of the soul are referred to as fragments. Larger parts are referred to as alters. Each alter can have a different and unique personality and their experiences pertain mostly to the spiritual world. There are structures inside the human soul that alters are familiar with, which serve as dwelling places for them. These places can be castles, hospitals, mansions, dungeons, fields, streams, woods or almost any setting you can think of. There are also places which lie outside of the soul, but still in the spiritual world that can be seen by alters. Alters are extremely aware of the presence of angels and demons, though due to demonic lies, they're often confused about the real identities of angels, demons, and Jesus. The ministry of inner healing and deliverance must take into account the reality of these inner worlds that are invisible to our physical eyes. Seeing in the spirit can be of great benefit to anyone who hopes to minister to people who have these conditions.

In her book *Regions of Captivity*, Ana Mendez Ferrell describes her discovery that the fragmented souls of people who suffer severe abuse and neglect are usually confined to prisons in various spiritual regions where they are abused and tormented by evil spirits. She teaches an approach to rescuing them that involves seeing into these dark places, and going there to open the prison gates and releasing the captives. This process is usually done with the help of angels who lead the way, deal with demon guards, and help unlock the prison doors. If God has called you to operate in a ministry such as this, it may require you to develop your ability to see what is happening in the spiritual world. Going into these unseen regions seems to be one strategy that God is using to help free people from the power of darkness.

I realize these experiences may lie outside the theological grid of understanding of many believers. To some they may seem like heresy and nonsense. To me they speak of the hope we have of healing and setting people free in ways most of us haven't considered. Some might object to such approaches on the grounds that they can't find anything like this being demonstrated in the ministry of Jesus. My response is that while Jesus healed and delivered untold thousands of people, in most cases no details were given about *how* He healed people. If He dealt with the same conditions we're dealing with today, who is to say He never healed a person's emotions or memories in ways similar to the ones described in this chapter?

I don't know anyone who is content with the understanding we presently have about healing. If one thing can be said about the current state of healing, it's that we still have much to learn. I believe God wants to teach us things that will help us set more people free from the bondage of the enemy and bring greater levels of healing.

Exercise

The next time you're in a setting where you have access to a group of people, ask the Holy Spirit to show you one thing about someone, concerning a need they have for healing. Look for images that would indicate the condition they have and look for direction from the Holy Spirit about how you might pray for their healing. Ask them if they would like to be healed and if they agree, pray for them as you are led. Record this encounter in your journal.

CHAPTER ELEVEN

Seeing in the Spirit and Deliverance

SETTING PEOPLE FREE OF DEMONIC oppression is one of the most important duties we have as Christians. But since demons are invisible (at least in the physical realm) it can be difficult to discern them. I'd like to share a testimony to illustrate how a well-developed ability to see in the spirit can assist you in setting people free of demons.

My EMT partner and I were on a transport of a patient who was at a doctor's appointment. We were sitting in the waiting room while the doctor examined our patient when I received a private message through a social network from a friend asking for help. My friend, who is a Christian, believed she had a demon and didn't know what to do about it. I sent her a message asking for more details. It turns out she had sensed the presence of the demon several days earlier. She had been rebuking it and commanding it to leave, but she wasn't making much progress. At the time she contacted me she could feel the demon in her upper chest and throat and felt as if it was about to leave, but she wanted a little help getting rid of it. The only problem was that she lived more than 1,500 miles away.

I got up from my chair in the waiting room and told my partner I'd be back in a few minutes. I went down the hallway and found the men's bathroom. I went in and locked the door. I closed my eyes and in my mind's eye, saw a representation of my friend sitting in front of me in a chair. I believed God wanted me to set her free of the demon in the same way I would if she were physically sitting in front of me. I sent her a message letting her know I would try to make the demon leave and asked her to keep me updated on what was happening through the private message.

I extended my arms as if I was placing them on her shoulders. In the vision in my mind, I could see my hands resting on her shoulders. I could not see the demon; I only saw my friend. I commanded the demon to come out of her in the name of Jesus. I checked my inbox to see if she had sent a message. She had. She said she could feel the demon moving inside of her and felt like she was going to vomit. I told her not to be afraid because the demon was definitely going to leave. I commanded the demon to come out several more times then checked again for a message. She said she suddenly felt the demon leave. It came up through her throat then she felt it leave through her mouth. She said she could not feel the presence of the demon any longer. She thanked me for helping her. I returned to the waiting room and took my seat beside my partner and continued waiting for my patient.

I receive dozens of prayer requests a week through e-mail and social media and this is how I usually pray for people. I close my eyes and wait to see what the Holy Spirit shows me. I often see a representation of the person I'm praying for either standing or sitting in front of me. Based on their prayer request and what I see happening in the vision, I pray for them until I see what appears to be the end result of what they need. The end of the prayer session is usually indicated when I see a sudden change in the vision or when it ends completely. These experiences are typical of the ones you'll have when you learn how to see in the spirit, and they'll help you minister deliverance to people over distances.

Discerning of Spirits

God's creativity is seen in all of nature. No two snowflakes are identical, and no two spirits are exactly alike. They are all unique and they all have certain weaknesses, strengths, and abilities. Each spirit is a specialist in one or more areas. Angelic spirits may specialize in things such as worship, healing, and control over the weather (see Rev 7:11, Jn 5:4, Rev 7:1). The same is true of evil spirits. Some demons specialize in physical affliction (see Lk. 13:11) and some cause people to be deaf and mute (see Mk 9:25). Some spirits specialize in emotional trauma, like the spirit that terrorized King Saul (see 1Sam. 18:10). Some specialize in divination, like the spirit Paul cast from the woman who followed him (see Acts 16:17-18).

One of the ways in which God helps us battle the kingdom of darkness is through the gift of "discerning of spirits" (see 1 Cor 12:10). The gift of discerning of spirits is most commonly used to detect demons and evict them. Demons are very good at concealing their presence. When a demon is exposed, it risks being removed and for this reason most demons do everything possible to avoid detection. Sometimes the presence of a demon in a person is obvious, but sometimes it is very subtle. Many people who have demons are not aware that they have them. Sometimes the only indication that a person may have a demon is a slightly odd behavior in one area of their life that corresponds to the demon's area of specialization.

It's difficult to remove demons from a person prior to detecting their presence and knowing something about their agenda. Even when they are detected, the process of evicting demons can be a long, fruitless effort that does not always result in the person being set free. Some who operate in deliverance would disagree with me, saying that removing demons is simply a matter of commanding them to leave by exercising the authority we've been given by Christ. They believe that when we tell a demon to leave, it has no choice to stay and it always leaves, without exception. They believe demons cannot resist our authority. Here's the problem I have with that position:

Those who say that demons cannot resist their authority never bother checking to see if demons actually leave when they tell them to. They operate on the assumption that a demon cannot possibly stay, so there's no reason to check to see if it's still there. It's my view that we ought to check to see if a demon actually left and this can be done by commanding the demon to manifest if it's still present. Try this a few times and you might be surprised at how often demons will manifest even after hours of commanding them to leave.

Since detecting demons is critical to removing them, the more people you have involved in the process who are able to sense demonic activity, the better your chances are of finding and removing them. Several people who operate in a strong ability to see in the spirit (or who can discern demons through others spiritual senses) may uncover and remove more demons than one person operating alone—especially if that person is not able to see well in the spirit. This is why it's wise to operate in teams when doing deliverance and healing.

Because discerning of spirits is a gift as opposed to an ability, it requires input from the Holy Spirit in order to operate. Discerning of spirits from visions involves the unveiling of the names of demons, their character traits and agendas, and areas of specialization. It's not unusual for a person to be afflicted by multiple demons and it's common for one demon to outrank the others. When we have a need to know these things, they may be revealed through all the spiritual senses.

The revelation of demons can be frightening to those who are not acquainted with them. When the Lord shows you people with all sorts of demons attached to them, chains, sharp objects, and devices they use to torment their victims, it can be frustrating if you don't know what to do with the information. It's not our responsibility to deal with every tormented person we encounter. There aren't enough hours in the day to battle every demon we see. Many people can't be set free until they've dealt with the things they've permitted to remain in their soul that allow the demons to be there in the first place.

Until we gain the full cooperation of the individual, it's useless to try to remove their demons. Even if you manage to make a demon leave an uncooperative person, it will likely return. God does not force deliverance on anyone. Most demonic oppression happens with the person's consent, even though most people aren't aware that they've given demons permission to harass them. Demons are allowed to harass us by virtue of the lies we believe about God or about ourselves, and through the power of verbal or mental agreements we make with enemy agendas. When we come out of agreement with lies and have our minds renewed to the truth, demons can be removed. Once we've found a person who is willing to be set free, the demons we are shown can be dealt with.

One of the most common spirits you'll see is a spirit of pain. I see them on or near almost everyone I pray with who suffers from any kind of painful ailment. These demons operate as spiritual hitchhikers, attaching to people as they pass by. When I see a spirit of pain it generally appear as a black shape with a cloud-like appearance. Spirits of pain seem to be about as numerous as mosquitoes. Depending on where you happen to be, sometimes it's impossible to avoid running into them. I've been "jumped" by these spirits often. I frequently see them attached to people who suddenly developed pain without having an actual injury.

One day my daughter was jumped by a spirit of pain while we were in an art gallery. She was minding her own business when she suddenly developed pain in her hand without injuring it. The circumstances seemed strange, so I closed my eyes and in my mind's eye, saw the presence of a spirit on her hand. It looked like a small, black, swirling cloud. Using my authority, I commanded the spirit to leave in the name of Jesus. The spirit didn't leave immediately. It traveled to her upper arm, then it went to her shoulder, and then to her back. This was evident because the pain in her hand moved to these parts of her body. I continued commanding the spirit to leave. After moving to various places in her body, it eventually left and didn't return, though I would imagine it probably attached to someone else after we left.

Many people who are attacked by these spirits assume incorrectly that they've done something to injure themselves or that they've suddenly become sick with some disease. When we assume that we have an injury, where no real injury exists, or when we assume that we have a disease without the actual disease being present, we are mentally coming into agreement with the enemy's agenda. The enemy would like us to believe the lie that we've been injured or developed a disease. When we believe such a lie, it opens the door for other spirits to pay us a visit.

I'm not dogmatic about this, but it seems as though the spirit of pain may act as a kind of doorkeeper for other spirits. A spirit of pain can gain entrance into our body and if it is not removed, it will invite other more dangerous spirits to take up residence (see Matt 11: 24-26). If we receive the first lie that the spirit of pain tells us, it's likely that we'll receive the next lie told by another spirit with a different area of specialization. As more spirits show up, they suggest more lies about why we're feeling these new symptoms. If we believe the lies, the spirits and the symptoms remain. This seems to be how spirits such as depression and sickness enter our lives and gain a foothold—the spirit of pain usually opens the door for them. The best strategy to stop evil spirits dead in their tracks is to be fully convinced in your mind that these spirits are intruders that must be removed.

When someone who feels aches and pains in various parts of their body undergoes testing but no underlying cause is found, they're usually given a diagnosis of fibromyalgia. This diagnosis is a way of categorizing pain that has no underlying physiological cause—at least none that can be found with conventional diagnostic testing. Recently, the Mayo Clinic has found that fibromyalgia symptoms often begin after trauma and the pain increases in severity over time. Many patients who suffer chronic pain have been healed of their symptoms after spirits of pain and emotional trauma were discerned and removed.

The key to defeating these spirits lies not in what you say, but in what you believe. You can rebuke and command evil spirits to leave all day long because it's what you've been trained to do. But if, in your heart, you believe that the pain you're feeling is real and if you believe it's connected to some underlying condition, it is unlikely that the pain or the spirit will leave. Demons are more sensitive to what you think than what you say. Your belief in the legitimacy of the symptoms plays into the agenda of the evil spirit and what you believe can allow it to remain there. What we believe about the afflicting spirit can either empower it or remove its power over us. The degree to which any spirit can influence us is determined by how much we believe what it says. This is true of both good and evil spirits. The consequence of believing what a demon says is that you'll come more under its influence. The consequence of believing what the Holy Spirit says is that you'll come more under His influence. Allow me to illustrate this principle:

In the fall of 2013, my wife developed lower back pain. MRI imaging revealed both herniated and bulging lumbar discs. We had two situations to deal with: The first was that she actually had a structural problem that needed healing. The second was that she had pain which may or may not have been an accurate reflection of the herniated discs. This may seem hard to understand, but the pain we feel is not always the result of an injury we have. People with obvious herniated discs on an MRI might not feel any pain at all. Conversely, people with normal MRIs often feel pain just as if they had a herniated disc. Some people experience "phantom" pain in limbs that were amputated years ago. Pain can be sensed in a part of the body that has no injury or where there is no longer even a limb.

My wife sought prayer for months and I prayed over her a number of times, but the pain in her lower back remained. One day she watched a healing testimony on my website from a woman who had believed lies about herself and about God's will for her healing. She was rebuked by a man who told her she had come into agreement with a bunch of lies from the enemy and he led her to renounce her agreement with them. She renounced her agreement with the lies and was miraculously healed. As my wife listened to her testimony, she realized that she had believed a lot of the same lies and agreed to the same wrong ideas about God and about healing. So my wife came out of agreement with the lies, received prayer, and was immediately healed. For this woman and for my wife, it was their wrong beliefs that kept them from being healed. If you're waiting on your own healing, consider the possibility that there is a lie you've believed that is preventing your healing from manifesting. Ask Jesus what the lie is and ask Him to show you the truth then believe it.

If you want to have success with deliverance by using your ability to see in the spirit, the most effective way is probably to work with a team. You can operate alone, but it seems to be safer and more effective if you can find a group of people to team up with. Many people who do deliverance regularly prefer to have at least two or three other people in the room who are proficient at detecting the presence of demons. It's important that the team members know and trust each other and are aware of each other's gifts and abilities. The operation of a team of people doing deliverance is not unlike that of a Special Forces unit.

Discerning the names and areas of specialization of demons takes a coordinated effort on the part of all the team members. Each person has something they are responsible for and they must communicate with the other team members what they are sensing and doing.

Many people who need deliverance have more than one demon. A good strategy for removing demons is to discern them one-by-one and remove them as they're detected. In some cases you will need to know the name of the demon before it can be removed, (see Mk 5:9) but that is not true in every case. Sometimes the name of the demon is the symptom it causes or the effect it has on the person. Some demons have names such as Pain, Depression, Infirmity, or Fear. Many times these demons can be evicted simply by announcing their name and telling them to leave in the name of Jesus. The revelation of the names of demons can come through what you see in a vision. You may also see devices in the spirit that need to be removed. In some cases, the demons will have different ranks. The lowest ranking demons are typically easier to remove, while the higher ranking ones are generally harder to remove. Sometimes you can get lower ranking demons to give you information about the higher ranking ones. (There is no loyalty among thieves.) In cases where there is a high ranking demon, if you're able to remove it, many times the rest of the demons will leave with it. The only way to become proficient at detecting and removing demons is to practice.

Author's note: I'm working on a book titled, *Inner Healing & Deliverance Made Simple*. You can subscribe to my updates on my website to be notified when it becomes available.

Exercise

The next time you are in a room full of people or perhaps with a friend or family member, ask the Holy Spirit to show you one evil spirit that is affecting someone else. Look for images that would indicate the kind of spirit they have and look for direction from the Holy Spirit about how you might pray to remove it. Ask the person if they would like to have it removed and if they agree, pray for them as you are led. Record this encounter in your journal.

Notes

Notes

CHAPTER TWELVE

Seeing in the Spirit and Your Personal Life

THE PREVIOUS CHAPTERS GAVE EXAMPLES of how seeing in the spirit can be used to help others. I don't want to give readers the impression that this ability is only intended for ministry. There is nothing sadder than a believer who can receive revelation from God for others, but not for themselves. The primary purpose for seeing in the spirit is to help us receive revelation about our own lives. God is forever about the business of helping us grow in intimacy with Him. Our ministry to others should result from the overflow of God's ministry to us. As He shows us things about our own lives, He also shows us things for others. In this chapter, I'll share some of the personal visual experiences I've had and explain what God was saying through them.

I often see visions while lying in bed at night before going to sleep. Most of them have to do with things that are on my mind. A couple of years after my father died I was lying in bed wondering what he was doing, where he was, and I guess I was just missing him. Apparently, God knew how I felt so he gave me a series of visions to encourage me. Perhaps it's why the Holy Spirit is called the Comforter. My grandfather was an avid photographer. I remember when I was growing up seeing many pictures of my dad and his family during the holidays and important times during their lives. I still have images in my mind of black-and-white photographs of my father and the people who were close to him. As I was lying in bed with my eyes closed, God began showing me a series of black and white photographs of my father that spanned his entire life. What struck me about them is that I had never seen any of them before. Some of the photographs were images of my father with his brothers and sisters, or my mother. Some were images of him with me and my brothers and sisters. Most of the settings were familiar to me.

After the vision of black and white photographs ended, I was given another vision. I saw a man dressed in a white suit walking on the shore of a lake. At first he was far off in the distance, but he was walking toward me. As he drew near, I thought that perhaps it was an image of me. The white suit that he wore looked exactly like the one I wore at my wedding, and the man resembled me. But as the vision continued and the man drew even closer, I was able to see that it was my father and not me. People have told me that I bear a strong resemblance to him. I sensed that he may have been walking along the shore of the sea of glass in heaven. My father always loved being around water. When I was a child we had a small boat. We spent many weekends exploring the lakes of Wisconsin with my father at the wheel of the boat. It was very encouraging to be shown a photo album of my earthly father that was taken by my heavenly Father.

Sometimes the visions that God shows me portray events from the past. One day I had been spending time listening to the voice of God when I suddenly saw a vision of horses running in a shallow, sandy riverbed. The imagery in this vision was crystal clear. It was like watching a high-definition video on a high-quality TV. In front of the horses that were running through the shallow water, I saw a man and woman who looked how I imagined Mary and Joseph might have looked. They were dressed in white robes and carried a child who was about two years old. The man was very thin. He had black hair and a long beard. As the vision played out, it felt as though I was seeing part of the journey when Mary and Joseph fled with Jesus to Egypt when he was a child. I'm not certain why I was shown this scene, but it may have been because God knew I was curious about this time in their lives.

Intercession

One night as I was lying in bed, God showed me a series of visions concerning my wife. I saw something like a castle of darkness around her. It was filled with skulls and demonic-looking objects. Feeling led to pray for her, I commanded the castle to be destroyed and asked God to build a temple of the Holy Spirit around her in its place. As the vision continued, I saw a temple being built around her, filled with light and fire. Then I saw a woman come out from the middle of the temple who was ablaze with fire. She ran into the darkness like a blazing warrior going into battle. On a different night God showed me a similar vision. That night as I closed my eyes, I saw her on a horse that had heavy armor fastened to it. My wife sat atop the horse in a full suit of armor and carried a heavy sword. She came charging out of a castle on horseback and rode across a wooden drawbridge at full gallop. She was followed by an army of soldiers on horseback that she led into battle. When I see visions like these, it gives me a direction to pray for her and many times instead of praying, I end up prophesying God's plans for her based on what I see in the visions. This is what I mean when I refer to ministering to others out of the overflow of God ministering to us. As I spend time with Him, He not only shows me things for myself, but for others, and I'm able to minister to them.

Many people receive visions from God in the form of grand panoramas that look something like a scene from a movie. These visions often involve a sensation of flying, where we're given an aerial view of a large section of land and sometimes we'll be shown an entire state or nation. The perspective may change from a wide angle view to a close-up, where our attention is drawn to an object or person. Frequently, these types of grand visions are a call to intercession.

I often see these types of visions when I'm attending a place of corporate worship. One day while I was attending a church service, during worship I saw many different visions of darkness and evil. I saw volcanoes erupting, clouds of ash and smoke ascending into dismal, dreary skies, darkness over the land, and eventually a capitol building came into view. The capitol was surrounded by darkness and evil. In the midst of all this darkness I saw the prophet Kim Clement standing illuminated in a shaft of light. He was singing, smiling, and prophesying to the capitol in the darkness. I knew this vision was given to encourage me to spend time praying for our nation and our political leaders.

I'm not sure why, but there does seem to be an increase of revelation and power for the miraculous when the people of God come together to worship Him. If your intercession depends on receiving revelation from God, it may be a good strategy to spend time in corporate worship receiving visions and other forms of revelation.

Spiritual Warfare

I have a couple of friends who became interested in the concept of gate-keeping. This was something the Lord suggested they pursue to gain greater understanding. One friend became weary of the demonic activity that was being played out in the lives of people in his neighborhood. One day God suggested that he establish gates in his neighborhood as spiritual entry and exit points. Late one night he decided to give it a try. He quietly went to several places that the Holy Spirit led him to and spoke prophetically to these points and established gates to deny entrance to evil spirits and allow entry to benign spirits. Within a few months, the demonic activity in his neighborhood ceased. One day he was walking with someone who did not know where he had established these gates. He told his companion there were gates at certain points and asked them to try to discern where they were. This person was able to detect one of the gates, by seeing its existence in the spirit.

Although visions can be a call to spiritual warfare, we need to be cautious not do battle outside of what God has authorized. One night as I was lying in bed, I felt led to pray against a demonic structure that the Lord showed me in a vision. I had no understanding of what the demonic fortress represented, or where it was located, but I made declarations that the fortress must be destroyed. I watched as the fortress was destroyed by fire, and saw demons fleeing from it. When there was nothing left but a smoking landscape, I felt good about this apparent victory so I decided to go for a bigger one. I had been learning about the orphan spirit, and decided I was going to pray against it. I closed my eyes and saw something like the blood-covered, spiked tail of a huge dragon. I prayed against it, but from what I could see, I was making no progress. I finally saw something like the eyelid of a large dragon. As I looked at it, the eye suddenly opened and looked at me with a menacing stare. I decided not to continue praying against it. If what I saw was a representation of the size and power of this spirit, it would probably take more firepower than I had to defeat it.

I think it's a dangerous policy to pick fights with spiritual powers when you don't have a clear and confirmed assignment from God against them. There are thousands of spiritual bad guys out there in every state and nation of the world that you could pick a fight with simply because they're on the wrong team. The fact that you see something in the spirit does not mean you have an assignment from God against it. You may not be properly trained and equipped to do battle against it. I believe that was the case with the spirit I was shown here.

I don't make a habit of picking fights with every spiritual being I'm shown, mostly because I know people who lived this way for a season and they found that it's a good way to get your head kicked in. When you go up against spiritual powers you're not assigned to fight and not equipped to handle, you're probably going to take a beating. John Paul Jackson's *Needless Casualties of War* is a good book on how to conduct spiritual warfare and intercession safely.

I had the opportunity to do some spiritual warfare near Sedona, Arizona, which is famous for its energy portals that are visited by curious seekers looking for spiritual adventures. On the way to Sedona, my companion, David Mclain, kept in contact by phone with a couple of friends who suggested we ask the Holy Spirit if He had any assignments for us in Sedona. We felt as though He did. As we kept in touch with our friends, who were in western Washington, they saw in visions a couple of angels who seemed to be bound by the enemy in the portal system near Bell Rock. After discussing what they saw and praying about it, we discerned that our task was to set the angels free and allow them to continue with their assignments. If you're wondering how an angel of God can be bound by the enemy in a portal, remember that the angel sent to bring revelation to Daniel was held up for 21 days by the enemy (see Dan 10:13).

This could have been a dangerous assignment, but I agreed to help with this mission for several reasons, which I'll outline for your consideration: First, I agreed to get involved because as a resident of Arizona, I represent God's government here. I'm not exactly sure how far my regional authority extends, but I'm confident that it covers the geographic area of my state. (Knowing something about your sphere of authority is important in spiritual warfare.) Second, we received confirmation from two trusted prophetic leaders who live outside the region about what was going on inside the portal. Third, I invited a seasoned warrior along on the mission who has been involved in this kind of warfare before. He's taken his share of beatings in the past, but he's learned how to conduct himself responsibly from those experiences. As a representative of my region, I extended him a personal invitation which allowed him to operate under my authority as a local representative. And last, I invited a few dozen prayer warriors on one of my social networks to cover us in prayer, even though I didn't tell them what we were doing. I would advise you to put a little thought, a lot of caution, and some serious prayer into your plans if you ever decide to try something like this.

After spending a few hours shopping in town, we headed to Bell Rock— the location of the largest energy portal. We believe that the portal system was created by God for good use, but since the creation of the portals, they've become polluted by the enemy, and we now consider them to be functioning under the control of the kingdom of darkness. So we decided to keep a safe distance while we engaged in warfare. We found a public parking area about a half mile away and surveyed Bell Rock and the much larger Courthouse Butte that dwarfed it, standing a few hundred yards to the east. We quickly and quietly spoke our decrees of freedom over the portal.

As soon as I began speaking, I sensed a strong presence of God's glory being released. The intensity of glory served as confirmation that we were indeed on the right assignment and over the target. As I closed my eyes, I saw a thick cover of dark clouds in the spirit overhead that was pierced by a brilliant shaft of light. An opening appeared in the clouds that gave way to a small hole of blue sky. I saw lightning strikes coming from the clouds above and a release of gold dust into what appeared to be the portal itself. I believe the release of gold dust into the portal was a symbolic confirmation that we had accomplished what we came for. It was all very interesting to watch. The prayers and commands only took a few minutes.

Seeing Into the Heavens

I began this book with the promise that I would show you how to develop a closer relationship with God by learning to see in the spirit. If supernatural experiences don't lead us closer to God, there is little reason to pursue them. One of the best things about seeing in the spirit is that it can lead us into a deeper, more significant relationship with Him. The writer of the book of Hebrews encouraged believers to draw near to the throne of God:

> *Let us therefore come boldly to the throne of grace, that we may obtain mercy and find grace to help in time of need.*
> HEB 4:16

For years I interpreted this passage symbolically. I never thought we could actually draw near to the throne of God in heaven until after we stepped into eternity for good. I now believe there is no reason why we can't literally approach the throne of God today to receive what we need directly from Him. The Bible not only says we *can* do this, but that we *should* do it, and that we should do it with boldness.

One day I was asked by a friend if I could help him enter into the heavens and perhaps see the throne room of God by faith. I agreed to at least try and see if we could do this as a group. My friend, my wife, and I took a seat in our living room and began worshiping the Lord. I closed my eyes and the first thing I saw was something like a stairwell leading upward that was illuminated at the top. Exerting my will, I ascended the stairwell and came out into a hallway that was illuminated by a soft, golden light. I went down the hallway—again by exerting my will—until I came to a portion of the hallway that had a window in the wall. Behind the window there was a soft, green light. Beside the window there was an open doorway. I stopped momentarily at the doorway then stepped through it into a large room that was dimly lit in a bluish light. In front of me, I saw a shallow pool of water. I could see that the water was only a few inches deep directly in front of me. I could not tell how deep it was farther from where I stood, nor could I see more than about 30 feet in front of me. I hesitated to go into the water, because I wasn't sure if it was safe. In my mind, I asked the Holy Spirit if it was safe to enter. I heard in my mind a voice that said, "Yes, it's safe." I entered the water and slowly walked forward. I say that I "walked" through the water because although it felt as if I was gliding along effortlessly, I could hear the splashing of water as if I were physically walking through it. This was an unusual thing for me. I don't normally hear things like this in the spirit, but this is proof that when we exercise our spiritual senses, they become sharper. As the water became deeper, I noticed a white light in front of me that was rapidly growing brighter. After a few seconds, I could make out a massive throne positioned directly in front of me and before long, I saw a being sitting on the throne that radiated the most brilliant white light I've ever seen. I looked around and saw a kind of amphitheater surrounding the throne with beings of light sitting in seats applauding the One who sat upon the throne. I knew I had somehow appeared in the throne room of heaven.

I kept my eyes closed and stayed in this experience for a few minutes, but I wanted to know if the others had seen anything like this. I opened my eyes and asked if they had seen anything. My wife and my friend both said they had not. Now I don't want to leave you with the impression that these experiences are only for certain people. They are for everyone who wants to have them. The reason they didn't see anything is because their ability to see in the spirit is still in the early stages of development. My wife is seeing more visions each day as she practices.

Some people might ask what the purpose is for having such experiences. Here is my answer: The earth and its inhabitants have very little ability to change the affairs of heaven, but heaven has a tremendous ability to change things here on earth. I believe Jesus really meant that our life's goal should to be to see to it that the things which happen here on earth reflect the way things are in heaven. The way in which we bring the things of heaven to earth is by visiting heaven, seeing how things are there, and finding ways to establish those same things here on earth. This is, and always has been, the ultimate will of God—that His will would be done on earth as it is in heaven. Since we've already been seated with Him in heavenly places (see Eph 2:6) maybe it's time we checked those places out to see what can be accomplished from the places where we've been seated. I plan to visit my heavenly home more often to learn about establishing His will on earth.

I hope this book has inspired to you to walk in the fullness of what God has called you to and I pray it will draw you closer to Him.

THANK YOU FOR PURCHASING THIS BOOK

For inspiring articles and an up-to-date list of my books, go to my website, **PrayingMedic.com**.

Other books by **Praying Medic**

Divine Healing
Made Simple

Hearing God's Voice
Made Simple

My Craziest Adventures with God
Volumes 1 and 2

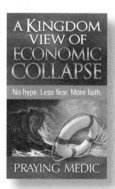

A Kingdom View of
Economic Collapse

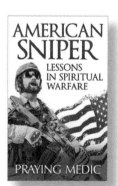

American Sniper:
Lessons in Spiritual Warfare

Emotional Healing
in 3 Easy Steps